WHAT'S IN THIS BOOK?

CW00953610

> *"It is very doubtful that we will look back and say it was wrong to talk directly and openly to children about difficult things."*
> Atle Dyregrov

OTHER HELPFUL RESOURCES

This book is primarily aimed at supporting children aged between five and 11; we have other publications aimed at those caring for younger or older children.

We have tried to keep this book a manageable length. When we have further supportive books, information or resources available, the links will be in a box like this one.

A CHILD'S GRIEF

Although we call this book 'A Child's Grief', it is really about **your** child's grief. You are probably reading this because a child or young person who you care about is grieving because someone important to them has died.

This person may also be someone important to you; if so, you are experiencing a double grief. Grieving for the person who has died and for the child who is bereaved. You may be a partner or ex-partner grieving while supporting your child; you may be a parent grieving for one child while supporting their sibling; you may be a grandparent grieving for your grown-up child while supporting their children and your grandchildren.

Every grief is individual – as individual as a fingerprint. Everyone will grieve in different ways and at different times, even within the same family.

You may be a professional concerned for a child who has been bereaved. Teachers and other school staff, health professionals, social workers and all members of the children's workforce (paid and voluntary) have a huge and important role to play in supporting children who grieve.

Whatever your role in this child's life, it is so painful to witness their grief. Your every instinct is to try to 'make it better', to protect them from sadness and smooth over any bumps and worries. However, the emotions we all feel when someone dies can't be 'made better'; but you can support children in their grief in many helpful ways.

The intention behind this book is to share what we at Winston's Wish have learnt about:

• **helpful ways of talking to children about death and dying**

• **funerals and other memorials**

• **how children grieve**

• **how a death can have a particular effect on an individual child**

• **what most helps children who are grieving**

• **how the future can still be full of hope**

We include some quotes from others who have had similar experiences and we suggest some creative ways to support children at this time. This book can be read through from start to finish but it is also possible to go straight to the relevant section for your situation at this time.

After supporting thousands of children and their families since we were founded in 1992, we know that, with the right support at the right time, children can find ways to live with their grief and go on to live rich and fulfilling lives.

Note on language:
The support and guidance offered is applicable to the death of anyone (not only parents or siblings) the child knows.

We use the term 'child' to include children and young people. When we refer to 'parents' or 'siblings', we are including the rich variety of family relationships and acknowledge the importance and value of other people in the child's life.

We mainly use the description 'person who has died'; this may feel rather impersonal and cool. However, we use this wide-ranging term to recognise that relationships can be complicated.

HOW MANY CHILDREN ARE BEREAVED?

Experiencing the death of someone important is a huge, life-changing and unique event to a child.

Because of medical and social advances with people living for longer, many people will now reach adulthood without experiencing the death of anyone close to them. A child living 50 years ago would have been more likely to have had family members die while they were growing up. That this experience has become rarer is, naturally, a good thing for families and yet it can make children who are bereaved feel more isolated, more alone with their grief.

Despite it becoming less common, around one child in 20 will have a parent die before the child is 16 years old. (That's the equivalent of one child in every class – although, of course, it doesn't even out like that across schools).

- **Around 110 children are bereaved of a parent every single day in Great Britain: that is four children every single hour facing the future without their mother or father**

- **many other children will experience the death of a brother or sister, a grandparent, close friend or teacher before they leave school**

- **most people known to a child will die from illness, whether their death is expected or sudden; this is true for parents and siblings and particularly true for grandparents**

- **about a quarter of these deaths will be unexpected**

- **at least three children a day are bereaved of a parent through suicide**

- **one child every day is bereaved of a parent through violence**

- **one study found that 78% of children said they had experienced a 'significant' or 'close' bereavement before they were 16.**

"I thought I was the only child without a dad. Other people at school didn't see theirs but at least their dads were alive. Somewhere. Mine wasn't." AJ

A Penny and D Stubbs, Childhood Bereavement: what do we know in 2015? London: National Children's Bureau.

L Harrison and R Harrington, Adolescents' bereavement experiences. Prevalence, association with depressive symptoms, and use of services. Journal of Adolescence 24(2): 159-169.

TALKING TO CHILDREN ABOUT DEATH

TALKING TO CHILDREN ABOUT DEATH

It's hard to talk about death to each other and even harder to speak to children about it.

Because having a relative die while you are growing up has become less common, we seem to have become rather out of practice at talking about death, especially with children, and the idea of doing so may make us anxious. We also have a natural instinct to protect them from harsh realities. At Winston's Wish, we hear from grieving children who tell us that they do want people around them to talk about the death of someone important and they do want their questions answered.

Children encounter death in stories from a very early age. Most five year olds will have watched *The Lion King*; most 11 year olds will have read some *Harry Potter*, for example. They may have had a pet die or found a dead spider and been curious.

Children develop their understanding of death as they grow. The process, over years, goes something like this:

- **the hamster isn't moving or eating, maybe he will tomorrow**
- **the hamster is this thing called 'dead' and we're getting a new one**
- **Grandpa is this thing called dead, but he'll still pick me up for football**
- **Grandpa is dead and I won't see or speak to him again**
- **old people die... this means that Granny will die one day**
- **all living things die... animals and birds and people**
- **all people die... this means that Mum and Dad and Mrs Wood will die one day**
- **all people die... and not only when they are old**
- **all people die... this means that I will die one day.**

You may be able to see where your child has reached in this process. By and large, children will have all the pieces of this understanding by the time they are nine or 10, although this will vary with their experiences and their developmental understanding. Put simply, they will understand that:

- **death is permanent and can't be reversed**
- **every human and every living thing dies**
- **death is caused by something: an illness, an accident or an event.**

Children also can use language which is more advanced than their understanding, so it is common for a child to tell their teacher: '*my gran died*' and then ask: '*but she'll still pick me up on Thursday, won't she?*'.

One helpful way of thinking about telling children and young people what has happened is to think of giving information in stages like building a jigsaw. Breaking the conversation up into smaller steps may help you to feel more in control and you can fit the steps to suit your child. Pieces of the whole picture can be added over minutes, over days or even months.

The pace of the stages will differ from child to child, due to their ability to understand as well as their willingness or reluctance to hear more information. For teenagers, you may be able to tell them everything you know immediately – the completed picture. For younger children, hearing that a special person has died may be all they can absorb at first.

Some young people describe getting stuck between feeling they want to know more but not wanting to upset their parents by asking questions. Not knowing can sometimes lead young people to make 'best guesses' or search online for information. Some guesses or information may be far from the truth. It may also be the case that details about the death are not known immediately and will not be known for months. It is helpful to children in these circumstances to know that you will tell them more when more is known.

1. Explain that the person has died

2. Give simple details about the death

3. Explain the death in relation to the child's life

4. Provide a more detailed description of how the person died

5. Explain what will happen next

This will probably be the hardest thing you ever have to tell your child. The most important thing is to say, simply, gently and clearly, that the person has died. You could start by saying something like: *'I have something very sad to tell you.'*

Follow this with the hardest part of the news: *'Daddy has died' 'Nanna died this morning'.*

As adults, we can find the words '**death**' or '**died**' very hard and blunt to say: but for children, these words are simply describing a circumstance that may be new to them. As a parent, your natural instinct will be to protect your children and avoid causing them distress. It's not a question of being brutally frank: what is important is to explain things using language children can understand. It is important that they hear the unique words that describe what has happened.

Depending on their age and level of understanding, children may understand what has happened or may need a little more information about what '**died**' means. For example: *'This means that his body stopped working. While we are alive, our lungs and heart and brain keep working without our even thinking about it. His lungs stopped breathing, his heart stopped beating and his brain stopped thinking. His body couldn't work anymore – and he died.'*

The next bit is to expand on what this means. For example: *'When someone dies, their body can't move or talk or eat anymore. This means that we won't be able to see or play with Dad again. It's not like he's in a different house or in a different town so we can't ring him up or video call him. It's so very sad.'*

Younger children will not understand that death is universal (that it happens to all living things) nor that it is permanent (that people can't come back to life). They might not understand that there is a reason why someone dies. Because they haven't yet developed a complete understanding of the fact that death is permanent, younger children may need to ask the same questions many, many times as they try to understand. (*'Is Jack coming back soon?' 'Where's Jack?'*) They may search for the person who has died in places they expect them to be.

"I found my granddaughter's questions about her mum's death overwhelming but then I realised how many I had too." Fiona

This is an opportunity to explain where and how the person died with a few, simple details.

It is important to check with the child what they understand about what has been said especially if you have used any words that might be new to them. For example:

- *'Mum was in a car that was hit by another car; Mum's body was hurt so badly that she died.'*
- *'You know Dad has been ill for a long time and the doctors have been trying so hard to make him better? Well, the illness he had was so serious that his body could not keep living and he died this morning.'*

When first told about a death, younger children may be mainly concerned with '**when**' and '**where**' the person died. It helps them to begin to imagine what has happened. The answer can be very simple.

- *'Grandad died this morning; he was in his lovely room at the hospice. His favourite nurse was with him.'*
- *'Imran died yesterday; I've been thinking about how to tell you. He was in his office at work.'*

Ask them if they would like to know more; even though it might be upsetting, it will mean that they are less likely to think about all the other possible ways they could have died. If children are not given information, they tend to fill in the gaps themselves and possibly jump to conclusions. There are examples on pages 50-51 of ways to talk about the death of someone through an accident or illness, or through suicide or violence. If children don't want to know more yet, remind them that this is okay and they can ask more questions at any point.

Slightly older children may also want to know '**how?**', and older ones may want to know '**why?**'.

People use various ways to discuss and begin to explain death with younger children – and you will probably find your own.

Sometimes, we suggest using the analogy of a hand and a glove. You and your child can each put a glove on one hand and challenge each other to do five things such as: open a door, pick up a toy, wave out of the window, turn the pages of a book, switch on the TV. Then you take off the gloves and challenge the gloves to do five things. When they don't move, you can explain that: *'The gloves only moved when fingers were inside them. And Gran's body only worked when her life was inside it. There was a part of Gran that was inside her body {her soul / spirit / love / specialness / uniqueness – whichever word feels right to you}. This made her body move and laugh and hug, rather like the way the fingers made the gloves do things. When she died, her body stopped working. It was like this glove – it couldn't do any of the things it used to do.'*

You could then, if you wish, add your own view or belief on what happens to that part of us after death. For example: *'I like to think that Gran's {soul / spirit / love / specialness / uniqueness} is {part of the natural world / in heaven / love all around us / etc}.'*

This is the opportunity for some immediate reassurance and comfort. For example:

- *'Even though this is the saddest thing to ever happen, we have got each other, and we will be OK…'*

- *'Dad loved you so much, he always looked forward to the weekend when he could spend more time with you.'*

- *'Aunty Brianna will pick you up from school and you'll come back here for tea as normal.'*

It's helpful for children to feel informed about what will happen next. For example:

- *'Granny will be coming to stay for a few days; she wants to make sure we are all looked after while we think about what has happened.'*

- *'It will be hugely different without Sam, but we'll keep on living here and you'll still go to school and see your friends.'*

- *'I'll get better at cooking and you can help me and we'll muddle through.'*

Older children may immediately consider the impact of this death on their own lives; realising that there are other changes up ahead.

12

4. PROVIDE A MORE DETAILED DESCRIPTION OF HOW THE PERSON DIED

What you say and when you say it will depend on your knowledge and understanding of your child and their developmental age and also on the nature of what has happened. Generally speaking, an 11 year old will have a different level of understanding to a four year old. Most people worry about telling children about how someone died, but if you say what has happened simply and factually, children and young people will be able to piece things together and start to make sense of what has happened.

So, take your time, explain in words your child will understand (there's some help on pages 15-18) and if you are introducing new words, explain what they mean. Children need time to absorb any information. Talking about how someone died will often open up more questions, though not always straight away. Consider this a good thing – one question asked out loud is one less question in someone's head

going unanswered. Children may ask the same question a number of times over the course of days, months or years. This is how they build their understanding and it's helpful to check that they have remembered things correctly.

Children may be concerned that the person who has died was in pain. It is important to be as honest and yet as reassuring as you can be. You might be able to say that you think the death was quick or that the person was unconscious or in shock so may not have felt pain, or that those treating them were able to give them medicine which helped the pain go away.

Although children may want to know more information, they can also become overwhelmed. It's important to reassure them that they are safe and after hearing something distressing, it might be helpful to do something comforting to relax and let the information 'sink in' gently.

5. EXPLAIN WHAT WILL HAPPEN NEXT

Older children will seek reassurance about the next steps facing the family. They will be aware that this death may mean significant changes in their lives: leaving their home, for example, or changing schools.

Younger children will also appreciate some reassurance that, even if there are major changes ahead, the family will come through.

As far as possible, involve children in conversations about the future. They might not be able to choose what happens but if they are informed, they will feel less as if everything is out of their control at a time when the world has become a very uncertain place.

THINGS TO REMEMBER

- talk to children using words they understand; give information to younger children a bit at a time

- try and encourage children to ask questions

- answer questions honestly and simply; talking about it won't make it worse

- accept that some things can't be 'made better'

- show willingness to talk about difficult things and use this as an opportunity to reassure

- if children are asking questions, it is a good thing – it shows they trust you and it is better than keeping questions and worries to themselves

- remember that 'super parents' or 'super teachers' don't exist: just do and say what you can

- don't be afraid to show children how you are feeling

"They had so many questions and I wasn't always sure of the answers but they accepted that… I always tried to come back to them once I'd thought about it." Ed

USING CLEAR WORDS

Sometimes, we can be tempted not to use words like: 'death', 'dead', 'died'. Because, as adults, these words are loaded with so much significance to us, we may be inclined when talking to children to use other words that seem to us to be 'softer' - as if the words we use can make what has happened less painful. The correct words used consistently and accurately help children understand that these are new words for circumstances unlike any other. Children, especially younger ones, can be very confused by expressions such as 'lost' or 'passed'. This confusion can lead the child to misunderstand, which makes it harder for them to make sense of what has happened. For example:

- 'We've lost your mum' (child may think: *'Well, look harder. Don't stop looking. Wouldn't you keep looking if you lost me?'*)

- 'Gran passed away…' (child may think: *'Passed? Like going past our front door? And has gone away somewhere? When will she be back?*)

- '… in her sleep' (child may think: *'Going to sleep is very dangerous. I'm not going to risk it. People like Gran just go away when they go to sleep.'*)

- 'Dad's gone to a better place' (child may think: *'Why didn't he take me too? He wouldn't choose to go somewhere else that's better without me.'*)

- 'Grandpa is in the sky' (child may think: *'Why can't I see him? How is he staying up there? Can we get a plane to bring him back?'*)

- 'Daisy is the brightest star in the sky' (child may think: *'No, that's Polaris. How can people become stars?'*)

Even a well-intentioned explanation of a deeply held and valued belief may be confusing. For example:

- 'Mum is in heaven now' (child may think: *'Why didn't she take me? They say it's nice in heaven and she's with Granny. I want to go too. Jake lives in Cornwall and you drive through Heaven to get there but Dad wouldn't stop.'*)

Sometimes, we use the proper medical terms without noticing that even these can confuse a child.

- 'Uncle Andy had a heart attack and died' (child may think: *'Attack? Someone attacked Uncle Andy? With knives? Was it the doctors?'*)

- 'Aunty Samira had a stroke and died' (child may think: *'She stroked my hair when I last saw her and I stroked her hand. I stroked the cat this morning – will it die?'*)

Sometimes even the right words are confusing without a bit of extra explanation.

- 'Dad's body will be buried…' (child may think: *'So what happened to his head and feet?'*)

As children grow, we name the new things they encounter. Having the right name for something helps a child begin to build their understanding of how this new thing is different. So, when introducing a new shape, we don't say **'It's like a square but it has three sides: we call it a three-sided square'**, we call the new shape **'a triangle'**. By saying that someone has **'died'**, the child can begin to recognise that this new word is linked to this new, huge thing that has happened to someone they know.

Children can still be offered your own personal, gentle, loving beliefs and explanations. These may make the reality and finality of death into something more comfortable for a child to consider. What can help, however, is expressing these as your **beliefs** rather than as **facts**. For example:

'You remember we talked about the fact that Mummy has died and this means we won't be able to see her, or hug her, or speak to her? I was out in the garden just now, and I was looking at all the blossom and feeling her very close to me. What makes you feel closest to her?'

'I believe that Justine is in heaven. It's hard to think about heaven because it's not a place we can visit or that people can send pictures or messages from. I think it's a place where people who have died are at peace with God. You may have some thoughts about it too.'

HOW TO TALK ABOUT DIFFERENT CAUSES OF DEATH

Once you have explained that someone important to the child has died, they may ask 'how did they die?'. There is more information on pages 50-51 about the possible impact on an individual child of different causes of death; the difference, for example between a long-anticipated death from a physical illness and a death by suicide. In this section, we are focusing on how to start talking about the different ways in which people may die.

EXPECTED

It may be that the person who has died has been ill for a long time and this has given you a chance to talk about what is happening as the illness progresses and a chance to offer your child gradual steps – or pieces of a jigsaw – towards understanding. It's also worth noting that, even when a death has been prepared for and expected, it can still feel very sudden and a shock to children. Children may have heard *'Lee is going to die'* and understood this as *'everyone dies: I expect Lee will be quite old when he dies.'*

You could say something like this: *'Do you remember how we talked about the illness Lee has and how the doctors have been working very hard to make him better? And that I said the other day that, sadly, the treatment wasn't working anymore – despite everyone trying so hard – and that Lee would die quite soon, maybe in the next few days? Well, I'm really sad to tell you this: Lee died this morning.'*

You could add: *'We all hoped that Lee would live until he was at least 100, but the illness was just too strong for his body, despite all that the doctors could do. This is rare and it's unfair that it happened to Lee, but everyone did all they could to help him to live.'*

> Our book **As Big As It Gets** is for anyone supporting a child when someone is seriously ill.

SUDDEN – ILLNESS

Sometimes, there is no chance to prepare for a death because the illness has not been known about: for example, someone may have a heart attack, brain haemorrhage or seizure. This is even more shocking when the person has previously appeared fit and well. You could say something like this:

'I have something very sad to tell you. Dad died this morning. It seems that his heart stopped beating – and when his heart stopped beating, his lungs stopped breathing and his brain stopped thinking, and so he died. This is called a 'heart attack' but nobody hurt him: his heart had a weakness that no one knew about. Dad died very quickly and the ambulance crew and the doctor who came said it didn't hurt him but there was nothing anyone could do to keep him living. His heart stopped.'

SUDDEN – ACCIDENT

Most parents who die before their children are 18 die from an illness. However, around one in five of these parents die due to an accident. Accidents may happen at work or when following a hobby, for example. Some people use the term 'accident' for a road traffic collision (which can be a bit uncomfortable for people who think another driver was at fault). You could say something like this: *'Lizzie went climbing this afternoon with her friends. They wanted to have another go at that steep face that they tried last week. It seems as if her foot just slipped as she was making a move and she fell to the ground. The fall was too far for her body to survive. Lizzie died before the ambulance arrived.'*

'I have something very sad to tell you. Mum was driving to work this morning when her car was hit by another car. We don't yet know how that happened. Mum's body was so badly hurt in the crash that she died. It was very quick and Mum wouldn't have felt any pain.'

SUICIDE

A death by suicide can bring additional complications for families: we talk about it as **'grief with the volume turned up'** because every emotion seems heightened – anger feels fiercer, fear feels larger, guilt feels sharper. Parents may feel particular anxiety in talking with children about suicide. Sometimes this is because a death by suicide can still attract a degree of stigma: it feels harder to say that someone ended their life than that someone died in a car crash or from cancer. Parents sometimes feel that they want to protect children from the knowledge that someone took their own life – maybe fearing that the child will feel the person 'chose' to leave them – and think it might be better to put off talking about how this person died until the children have grown up. We believe that children need to trust their parent(s) and hearing the truth from them (not in the playground, on social media or unexpectedly in the future) builds and cements this trust. How much you share and when will depend upon your individual child (and it is difficult to talk about suicide with children who don't yet understand about death and dying). It may be easier to break it down into a few stages – with a younger child, this might take a few weeks; with an older child it might be within the one conversation.

Our Freephone Helpline can help you think through talking with children about a death by suicide; our team can also help you with words for the various ways people end their life.

As an example of the complete set of stages of explanation, you could say something like this:

'I have something very sad to tell you. Dear Uncle Mike died yesterday. I heard last night and I wanted to understand a bit more about what has happened before I told you.'

'It seems as if Uncle Mike had an illness that we didn't know about. It's not like an illness or pain that people can see on the outside. The illness changed the way he thought and felt, and it made him very sad – a very dark sort of sadness. Not the sort of sadness you feel when I say you can't have more cake, but deep sadness caused by this illness which made Uncle Mike feel that he could not go on living.'

'It is hard to stop a body living; our hearts and brains and our bodies keep working without us thinking about it. So, he had to do something to make his body stop working.'

'What he seems to have done is to stop himself breathing which meant his heart stopped and his brain stopped and he died. He stopped himself breathing by putting something tight around his neck – as you know, that is a very dangerous thing to do.'

'It's hard for all those who knew Uncle Mike to understand why we didn't know and why he didn't reach out for help. I think it's a bit like being in a room which has dozens of doors. If you and I were in that room, feeling mentally strong and well, we'd just walk up to any of the doors and find out that it was open – and behind each door there'd be an idea or something that could help. But the illness inside Uncle Mike's brain made him think that all the doors were locked so he didn't or couldn't try the door handles. Maybe he didn't even see the other doors. He could just see one door open – the one that led him to end his life.'

'We all have a sort of tower inside that keeps us strong and healthy. Sometimes, some people like Uncle Mike have an illness like depression that can eat away at the cement holding their tower together and it becomes more like a Jenga tower than a tower block. People don't notice this from the outside but the tower becomes very wobbly. Stuff that happens can knock bricks out of the tower and then pressures pile on top – like the bricks pile on top in Jenga. And you never know what's going to bring the stack tumbling down. It's why we have to make really sure that our own inside towers are strong and safe and holding us up: and our 'cement' is in good condition.'

Our book **Beyond the Rough Rock** is about supporting children bereaved by suicide.

"Being honest about their dad has made it easier for us to focus on the memories that will help us all move forward." Shelley

MURDER OR MANSLAUGHTER

When someone has been killed through murder or manslaughter, every feeling and every reaction of those left behind will be intensified. Children may experience profound and lasting shock, enormous anger at what has happened, huge rage at the person who caused their relative to die, and deep fear at the perceived insecurity of the world around them.

Sadly, in many cases, the person who caused the death is also known to the child, resulting in great confusion and a double loss, for example, if one parent kills the other and is then imprisoned and out of contact. The world feels even less safe when a stranger is responsible for the death or when the killer has not been found.

Oddly, children and young people may be more aware of murder and manslaughter as a cause of death than almost any other; while at the same time, society finds it very hard to think of the impact of a death by violence on the family of the person who died. Yet, many characters in children's fiction have been bereaved through violence (Harry Potter, Simba the Lion King, Batman); murder mysteries are popular, and many animated cartoons and games involve repeated violent deaths.

Sometimes after such a death, the child may have to move house, school, area – away from familiar and comforting places and routines. It can be difficult to live with grandparents who are mourning the loss of their own child (the child's parent) and who are unable to forgive the person who killed them (who may be the child's other parent).

To explain what has happened, you could say something like:

'Sometimes, in very, very rare circumstances, something happens to change the way someone is thinking and they do really bad things that they would not normally do. Sometimes this means they also hurt someone more than they meant to. It seems as if this is what happened to {name of the person who caused the death} and that means they hurt Ella so badly that she died...'

'...The police will keep him in prison. He can't hurt anyone else.' or *'...We may never know why this happened but the police will keep looking for whoever did this to Ella.'*

DISASTER OR TERRORISM

It's a rare event, but occasionally a member of the public is caught up in a tragic event. This might be a fire, a natural disaster or an act of terrorism. The explanation can be basic, especially for young children. You could say something like:

'What I am going to tell you is very difficult to explain. Dan has died. You remember everyone was saying that something was going on in town? Something very bad and very sad has happened. It seems that a person suddenly started shooting people on the street and sadly Dan was one of those people. He was hurt so badly that he died right there before the police and ambulance people could reach him. When someone is shot, the bullet from the gun goes into their body and causes them to bleed a lot. Our bodies need blood to make all the parts work properly. If someone loses too much blood, their body stops working and they die. Other people were hurt and some have also died. The police have caught the person who was shooting. It is very unusual that something like this happens and it is terrible that Dan happened to be there just then.'

Our book **Hope Beyond the Headlines** is about supporting children bereaved by murder or manslaughter.

EXPLAINING CHANGE – AN ALTERED FUTURE

Children can find change difficult to contemplate and also to experience – and the death of someone close frequently brings many changes. The most obvious change is that the person who has died can no longer be an active part of the child's life. Other changes may involve where a child lives or goes to school, who is around at bedtime and on the school run, and how much a parent can support the child because of their own grief. One change, such as a new house, can bring many more.

Your child will appreciate knowing as much as you feel appropriate to share about:

- **what has happened**
- **what is happening**
- **what will happen.**

Feeling better informed and having things explained in simple, age-appropriate language helps them to feel a little bit more involved. In this way, they feel a little more secure.

After someone important has died, children appreciate reassurance that balances honesty with optimism. They may, for example, worry that you will also die soon. It's important to reassure while not making impossible promises that they may immediately challenge. One thing that seems to provide reassurance is to provide mental images of you in the future for your child to hold on to. You could say something like:

'I have every intention of living until I'm at least 111 years old. I'm planning on being around to see not only your children grow up but also your grandchildren. And how I will spoil them! So many sweets! I hope to live until I'm much older than {the Queen or anyone older who the child knows}. And I intend to start a new career as a professional dancer when I'm 70 and as a footballer when I'm 80. What do you think I should do when I'm 90?'

> *"I kept repeating it will be ok, we will be ok. I think I was telling myself more than the children."* Anne

Short term reassurance when apart can also be provided by mental pictures of being together later. These images seem to reassure more than something harder to imagine such as: 'I'll see you at the end of the day.' You could say something like:

'When I pick you up, would you remind me we need to buy potatoes.' Or *'When we go to town on Saturday, we must get a card for Albie's birthday.'*

Ideas of reassurance activities such as those on pages 58 and 59 can also help. Even a simple kiss made from two stitches sewn into a school top can be held discreetly when a child is feeling a bit wobbly.

Sometimes we all need a reminder that things will be OK. They **will** be different, and some things **will** change. Some differences will be more difficult than others but a positive, even if altered, future is possible for everyone. It's a little like the words in the 'Bear Hunt' story by author Michael Rosen: *'We can't go over it, we can't go under it, we can't go round it… we've got to go through it.'* (And it helps if we hold hands while we do.)

QUESTIONS CHILDREN MAY ASK

It is really important to answer children's questions as openly, honestly and straightforwardly as possible. If you feel that the answer to a question is too much for the child to hear right now, say so; although do bear in mind that children usually only ask questions when they want to know and can handle hearing the answers.

It's okay not to have all the answers straight away: if you don't know the answer, you can always say you will try to find out. It is almost always a good idea to say something like *'That's a very good question. While I think about my answer, what do you think the answer is?'* However, it is also really helpful to think through your answers to some common questions so you are prepared when they come.

Here are some examples of questions that may come up when someone has died. Of course, questions and concerns are as individual as the person asking them… and our suggested replies are only meant as general guidance.

- **Will you die too?**

    'I have every intention of playing with your grandchildren, not just your children! I will do all I can to remain healthy and to go on looking after you until you are old yourself!'

- **What will happen to me if you die?**

    'It is really unlikely that I will die before you are grown up, but if I were to die, Martine and Peter would want you to live with them and their children so that you could keep going to the same school and still see your friends.'

- **Will I catch this too? Will I die?**

    'You can't catch this illness. That's not how it works. It is really unusual and sad that Mum had this illness – most people die when they are very old. I expect you will live to be at least 111!'

- **Did I make this happen? Is it my fault?**

    'Nothing you did or didn't do; nothing you said or thought – or didn't say or didn't think – made this happen. It's no one's fault.'

- **Why couldn't they make her better?**

    'The doctors worked very hard to make Mum better. Sometimes this happens; not everyone can be made well again.'

    'Her body was hurt too badly to keep on living. Her heart stopped, her brain stopped and she died.'

- **Does it hurt to die?**

    'No, it doesn't hurt to die and it doesn't hurt to be dead.'

- **Why didn't someone else die instead?**

    'It seems so unfair, doesn't it, when we loved her so much? But, sadly, her body stopped working. Nobody else could take her place. We all wish she hadn't died.'

- **Can I see Mum again?**

    'It's very sad but no, we can't see her again. But we can look at her photos, tell stories about her and remember her every single day.'

- **Can I still go to football?**

    'We'll do everything we can to keep things ticking over as normal. Jake's dad has offered you a lift every week – and he'll make sure you and Jake get something to eat beforehand. He says he's very good at making chips.'

- **Do you still love me?**

    'I love you with all my heart. Sometimes I am so sad about what has happened that I forget to say it – but I will never ever stop loving you.'

BEYOND WORDS

A big part of how you and your children share your grief may be through hugs and tears – not words. Additional, non-verbal comfort can be very helpful when someone has died. This might be from hugging old, favourite toys or being wrapped in snuggly blankets. Sometimes reassurance can come from having a slice of toast cut into a heart shape or a small picture placed in a lunchbox.

Children, of course, don't only listen to what we say, they also watch what we do. If we hide all of our feelings and try to put on an unchanged 'face' to children, they can become very confused: *'Daddy died but Mummy doesn't seem sad.' 'Grandpa keeps baking and telling jokes so maybe I shouldn't be upset that Grandma died?'* If children see you being sad, or being cross, they learn that it is safe to feel and express large emotions. And when they see you still able to make the tea or put on a load of washing, they are learning that it's safe to express their feelings because they, too, will be able to come through them to somewhere else. Children never 'want' us to get upset, but they 'need' to see us get upset and then smile and have a biscuit while playing with Lego.

In all of these ways, through what we say and how we respond to their questions, we are giving children the information they need to start to understand what has happened, and how they and those around them may react to this huge change in their lives.

"It took a long time to realise that this wasn't a test – it was the rest of our lives now. But we play as a team (most of the time!)" Mo

"*Some people come into our lives and quickly go… They stay in our lives for a while, leave footprints on our hearts and we are never, ever the same.*" Flavia Weedn

SAYING GOODBYE

PREPARING TO SAY GOODBYE

In some ways, this section is misnamed, because - in so many important ways – the person who has died will continue to be a part of a child's life and memories. We are using the term '**goodbye**' here to include the kinds of events (seeing the body, the funeral, memorial services) that take place after someone has died.

We recognise that, depending on faith and cultural practices and beliefs, there may not be much time to prepare a child for what happens or to include them after someone dies.

It is important to keep making clear that the person's body cannot feel anything nor do anything. If, for example, the body is in a funeral home, you could explain that the person who died is not cold, they're not hungry, they're not lonely.

Once in a while, a child is confused when we talk about a person's 'body'; it's worth checking that they realise you are talking about the whole of the person's body, including the head and legs.

SEEING THE PERSON'S BODY

The decision whether or not to see ('view') the body of the person after they have died will be a personal one: this is just as true for children as it is for adults. Often parents and carers believe that it would be too distressing for a child – or for themselves. Or they think that the final image of the body of the person who has died will block out other images. Preparation is the key. Often a child's imagination about what someone will look like after they have died is worse than the reality. If children have clarity, they often can manage this very well. Having a mental image of a person's body, alongside other images and memories, doesn't have to be a negative thing, and we encourage conversations both about what the person looked like after they died, as well as the conversations about what they were like when they were alive. This balance is important for children to be able to carry the positive memories alongside their grief and loss. Mental images of the person alive will, in time, be more powerful than the images of them after death.

Seeing the physical body of the person who has died can help a child begin the process of understanding that death is final and it can also play a very valued part in saying goodbye.

For a child to be able to make this choice, they will need some clear information and some preparation for what seeing the person's body will actually mean.

HOW TO PREPARE CHILDREN TO SEE THE BODY

If your child decides they do want to see the body then there are some important ways you can help to prepare them.

- make sure your child has understood that the person has died. If a child is asked, *"do you want to go and see Uncle Jack?"* then they will, of course, say that they do, as they may not understand that it is his body they will be seeing

- make sure to explain that the person's body will look and feel different to the living person's body. Their body has stopped working, their heart has stopped beating and their brain has stopped thinking. Although their eyes will be closed, they are not asleep. For example: *'Amy's body has stopped working and that makes her look different to when you saw her last week. Because her heart isn't beating any more, her blood isn't being pumped around her body, so she looks quite pale. Her skin is also quite cold to touch and a little harder than it was when she was alive. You can touch her, though, and kiss her if you want to.'*

- sometimes, a person's face or body is hurt too badly to be comfortable to see. If this happens, the funeral director may be able to make it possible to hold the hand of the person who has died – or even the foot. For example: *'Patrick's body was hurt very badly when he died. Patrick didn't feel that pain, but it does make his face look very changed from how you remember him. I know you want to say goodbye, so I've asked the funeral directors to make it possible for us to hold one of his dear, beautiful hands instead of seeing his face. His face and the rest of his body will be covered up with a piece of material.'*

- describe what else they might see, especially how the body will be presented. This includes describing whether the body will be on a table or inside a coffin and what clothes the person will be wearing. For example: *'Mum will be lying in a wooden box called a coffin. The lid will be open so we will be able to see her body and she will be dressed in the outfit that you helped to choose.'*

- describe the room where the person who has died will be. If possible, you could visit beforehand so that you can describe it. For example: *'It's a little chilly in the room but there's a big window looking out on some trees. It's painted a nice pale blue colour and it doesn't smell at all funny.'* Or if possible, take them to the room before the body is there so they can get a sense of what it will be like

- reassure them that it is their decision and that they can change their mind. They can stand at the door and look from a distance or they can go close and touch the person – it is their choice. Remind them that they can leave at any moment and that they can change their mind at any point. It would be helpful to have another adult on hand for support if they wish to leave

- take something to leave with the body. This could be a card, a photo, a flower. This also helps if your child decides not to go in – they can still feel that they have done something for the person

- reassure them that there is no right or wrong choice, and if they choose not to go that does not mean that they didn't love the person who has died. This is especially important when there are siblings, some who want to view the body and some who don't

- if your child does not want to see the person's body but does want to have some time with the body before a funeral, they may find it easier to spend time with the coffin with the lid closed.

'Wayne's body was so badly injured I let the girls know that we would only be able to see part of his body. We organised for his body to be covered, but his hands and arms were not covered so the girls could hold his hand. I must admit I thought it was going to be horrendous, but it really wasn't and the girls said how comforting it was to be able to touch him one last time.' Katie

ATTENDING THE FUNERAL

Parents may be unsure about whether to include children in a funeral; sometimes this is because of cultural or religious beliefs that need to be followed. But sometimes, parents are unsure because of their anxiety over the impact attending a funeral might have on a child.

Your children are your children; you know their individual needs, worries, strengths. At Winston's Wish, we have listened to and supported thousands of children and young people across the years. We have spoken to children who chose to attend the funeral of someone important and were glad they did. We have spoken to children who chose not to attend and had no regrets. We have never spoken to a child who attended a funeral and wished they hadn't… but we have spoken to very many children who did not have the chance to attend and deeply regret not going.

Children really value being given a choice over whether or not to attend. Being at a funeral can help them to begin to accept the reality and finality of the death and begin to understand a little more about what has happened. Being part of what is happening can help children feel included in sharing this important memory with those they love. Children understand and appreciate sharing in the sadness of people close to them: after all that is what they are feeling too.

Sometimes, it is not possible for children to attend the funeral; for example, it may take place in another country. There are other positive ways in which they can be involved, for example, through helping to plan the funeral, choosing a particular piece of music to be played or a poem to be read. They may wish for something to be put in the coffin on their behalf, for example, a picture, flower or toy.

One significant factor that may affect a younger child's attendance at a funeral is if they – and you – feel their presence is welcome there. If there is going to be tension between family members or past partners (as opposed to natural sadness), they will pick this up and feel more distressed by the atmosphere than by what is happening.

WAYS TO EXPLAIN A FUNERAL TO CHILDREN

To help a child or young person decide whether or not to attend a funeral, it helps for them to have clear information about what will happen, who will be there, how people may react and whether the funeral will involve a burial or a cremation. Here are some examples of what you might say:

'After someone dies, we have a special service called a funeral. A funeral is a chance for people to say goodbye to the person who has died. It's also a time for people to be with the family of the person and show them their support. The service is usually held in a special place (for example: church / chapel / synagogue / mosque / natural burial ground). Usually, there is some music, some prayers and people say what they remember about the person who has died.'

'On Thursday, we're having Dad's funeral. His body will be there in a special box called a coffin and afterwards, his body in the coffin will be (buried / cremated). Many people will be there – all of our family and so many of our friends and Dad's colleagues. People will be upset because it is so very sad that Dad has died but they will also be talking about their memories of him.'

HOW TO EXPLAIN BURIAL AND CREMATION

Adults sometimes wonder if children will be concerned or even frightened by discussion of what actually happens to the body during a funeral. In our experience, simple, straightforward explanations answer children's natural questions and can be reassuring. Here are some ways of explaining what happens:

'Remember I was talking about a funeral being a chance to say goodbye to the person who has died? Although the person has died, we treat their body very respectfully and gently, even though the person can't feel what happens to their body after they have died. Around the world, people have different traditions for what happens. Here, we either 'bury' or 'cremate' someone's body.

'Bury' means that the coffin with their body inside will be gently placed in a hole in the ground and covered in soft earth. This is called 'a grave'. People then might plant flowers to grow over the grave and sometimes they might come to visit the grave to spend some time thinking about the person who died.

'Cremate' means that the coffin with their body inside will be gently placed in a hot fire which turns it all into soft, powdery ashes. When these are cool, people sometimes scatter the ashes at a place that was special to the person who died, or people might keep the ashes at home in a special container called 'an urn'. People sometimes turn some of the ashes into something that helps them to remember the person who died.

Remember that the person's body can't feel anything anymore, so this doesn't hurt them.'

If it fits with your own beliefs, it will help if the child has had some preparation about the difference between the body of the person and the part that made them who they were. Some people call this a soul, or a spirit, or love, or *'what was special about Daddy'* or *'what we will remember about Daddy'*.

If you have used the idea of a glove and the fingers inside to explain death and dying (see page 11), you can use this to explain that the body doesn't feel pain.

'Suppose I put the glove in the ground, it wouldn't hurt the glove, would it? Or if I put the glove on a bonfire, it wouldn't hurt the glove. It would only hurt if fingers were still inside it.'

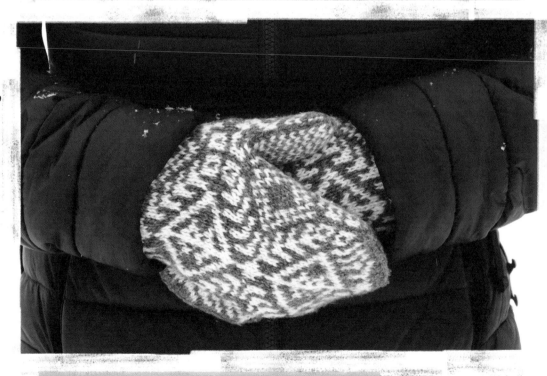

"She keeps the order of service booklet in her memory box along with a dried rose. she put one from the same bunch on her grandad's coffin during the funeral." Jude

HOW TO PREPARE CHILDREN FOR A FUNERAL

- remind children that the funeral is a chance for everyone who cared about the person who died to say goodbye and to show their support to that person's family

- offer them clear information about what will happen and in which order (for example: the service, the coffin leaving to be cremated or the burial, the reception (*the cup of tea and piece of cake afterwards*))

- explain again (as above) about the fact that the person has died; their body will not be aware of anything that is happening

- say who you expect to be there and prepare them for the way people might react. They may see adults in deep distress – this is a natural response to the huge thing that has happened

- also, explain that people can't help saying something like '*How lovely to see you*' when meeting a cousin; this doesn't mean they are happy and enjoying the occasion

- some children can be shocked that the funeral reception (sometimes called 'the wake') afterwards can feel more like a party. Explaining that adults are sharing memories of the person who died and these include happy memories... it means they are celebrating the person who was alive, not that they died

- prepare them for some of the things that adults may say to them. For example, boys may be told after the death of their father that they are the 'man of the house now'. Remind them that they are not; other adults will take on his responsibilities

- have a special person who is there to act as key supporter for the child; this could be someone like a grandparent or family friend. This person can leave with the child if it becomes overwhelming, be alert to how they are feeling, and help out with tricky conversations with distant relatives. This frees you to be able to participate fully in the funeral for your own sake

- sometimes, a child will choose (or you might suggest) attending parts of the funeral – for example, the service and the reception; others might find the reception too much

- think about ways the child can be involved in a funeral. This may be through planning the service, choosing music, choosing the clothes the person will wear. Some children may want to say a few words they have written or read a poem. Reassure them that someone else can take over if it becomes overwhelming

- children may wish to have something special placed in the coffin, for example a drawing, a photo, or something linked to a shared memory

- keepsakes from the funeral service can be very meaningful for children. For example, some flowers from the tributes to press and keep; a leaf from one of the trees in the grounds; a pebble from the surrounding area; the order of service

- let them know that they can change their minds at any time about attending the funeral or about reading. Check that they are happy with the choice they've made – but not too often, since children may say what they think you want them to say to please you

- give plenty of reassurance that they can still be involved and participate in saying 'goodbye' even if they choose not to attend and that they won't be criticised if they don't go to the funeral

"They both wanted to be involved. Callum wrote a beautiful speech and Iain wrote a stunning poem but asked Callum to read it for him. Peter would have been so proud." Sylvie

CAPTURING MEMORIES

A funeral offers a valuable opportunity to ask those who attend to contribute towards a store of memories and stories for the children to explore over time. Stories about the person who died play a crucial part in maintaining memories for children.

Sometimes, people provide cards on which those present at the funeral can jot down memories, thoughts, anecdotes. However, people usually write much more if they are encouraged to take the cards away and send them back to the family afterwards. Those who can't attend can have the memory card emailed or posted.

These stories and memories become increasingly precious to children and have a particularly important part to play for children who are very young when their special person dies. When few memories remain – or when there are none – stories take their place in building up a picture of the person.

These stories and memories can be kept in a box or jar to be drawn from.

Here's a starter that can be adapted:

> To all the family and friends of _____ (first name of the person who has died)
>
> I knew them _____ (e.g. 'when we worked at the shop'; 'from the pub')
>
> I will always remember _____ (some general observation, e.g. 'their generosity'; 'their terrible jokes')
>
> In particular, I remember _____ (some specific memory/ memories, e.g. 'the day we missed the bus and had to walk home'; 'her teaching me to swim')
>
> They were good at _____ (something either physical: 'crazy golf' or, if possible, some special quality: 'making people happy')
>
> Always know that _____
>
> Thinking of you at this time.
> _____ (Name – and contact information if possible)

WINSTON'S WISH WW
Giving hope to grieving children

"She loves getting out the box and reading stories about her mum. Some people also sent photos that I'd never even seen and someone drew an amazing picture of them camping at a festival in the rain." Sam

OTHER WAYS TO SAY GOODBYE

If it is not possible or children choose not to attend the funeral, there are other positive ways in which they can be involved in saying goodbye. Perhaps they could be involved in the planning of the funeral, choosing a particular piece of music to be played or poem to be read. They may wish for something to be put in the coffin, for example, a picture or card. Sometimes a child might choose two identical objects, such as a soft toy, send one to be put into the coffin and keep one for themselves.

You could hold a small alternative ceremony just for you and them, maybe lighting a candle or planting a tree together, and saying a few words.

MEMORIALS AND CELEBRATIONS OF LIFE

Not all funerals are sombre occasions; there has been a recent trend for funerals that are more colourful and celebratory. Sometimes, people assume that these are easier for children to attend. In practice, children can feel uncomfortable and bewildered at this type of funeral: why aren't people feeling sad that their important person has died? Some explanation about celebrating the person's life rather than that they died will help a child who is confused.

It can help if the **'saying goodbye to someone who has died'** and the **'celebrating the person who lived'** events can be separated by a little time. This also gives a chance for the family, including the children, to take their time to plan for a special memorial service.

A memorial service can also take the place of a funeral for children who could not or who chose not to attend. This might be linked to the date of death, or to the person's birthday. Also, if the funeral happened some time ago and children now regret not attending, it is never too late to have a memorial or other ceremony that includes and involves them. There are some ideas on p72-73.

"We helped Millie to buy two soft toys that were exactly the same – one was buried with her dad's body and she keeps the other one to feel close to him." Kelly

"A child can live with anything as long as he or she is told the truth and is allowed to share with loved ones the natural feelings people have when they are grieving." Eda LeShan

HOW CHILDREN GRIEVE

IN THE FIRST DAYS AND WEEKS

Children will respond to the news that someone has died in many different ways depending on their level of understanding, their age and their temperament.

The very first reaction can seem surprising. After hearing: *'I have something very sad to tell you, Grandpa died today'*, a child's response may be to ask: *'What's for tea?'* or to ask: *'Can I watch the TV?'* or ask to play their favourite game. People can be a bit shocked by this sideways swerve into activity yet such reactions are very common and in no way reflect a child's true character. It's maybe some deep, primitive level of survival – instinctively to push away what is too hard to bear and to focus on temporary distraction instead. Equally, a child may be immediately overwhelmed by grief, unable to stop shaking and crying. All of these – and more – reactions are natural and do not mean your child doesn't care or is overreacting.

Parents tell us that children at any age may become very distressed or may seem matter-of-fact. Some may immediately focus on the details of what has happened, others may not want to know. Some children will worry about the future, some will worry about other members of the family, some will worry about telling their friends.

Children grieve in different ways according to their stage of development in terms of what they understand, what they feel and how they behave. They also grieve in differing ways according to their own personalities and life experiences.

All people, whatever their age, have many different and intense feelings when someone dies. Children are just the same but their ability to understand and use words to describe their feelings will vary. It can help if adults help by describing some of their own; this can be particularly helpful if your child struggles to recognise their own and others' feelings. **'I am quiet because I am feeling rather wobbly when I think about Mummy Jo dying and I am very sad, which is why I am crying. I'll be OK in a few minutes and then we can build some Lego.'**

"Our children reacted so differently. From the minute I told them their dad had died, Izzy shared every single feeling, thought and question. Patrick said nothing about it for weeks." Bryony (of her 8-year old twins)

People have individual ways of expressing their feelings. Some people find it very hard to cry or to put into words how they are feeling: it doesn't mean that they aren't as distressed as someone who can't stop crying. You may find that other people try and suggest how you or your child are feeling: ('*you must be feeling very…*') or even tell you to grieve in a particular way ('*you need to…*'). Try to remember that everyone, including you, grieves differently. There's no set of 'rules' or 'stages' and no 'right' or 'wrong' way to be feeling.

People often ask: '*how are you feeling?*' and it can be impossible to answer; it's even harder for a child to answer. When someone dies, you can be left with an overwhelming jumble inside and to name the feelings people have when they grieve for someone is a little like listing every emotion that can be thought about and named. These are some of the most common ones for children to feel; they are listed alphabetically as there is no particular order or priority to how anyone may be feeling.

- **Anger**
- **Anxiety and fear**
- **Arguing**
- **Avoidance and denial**
- **Confusion and bewilderment**
- **Disbelief**
- **Guilt and feeling to blame**
- **Hollowed-out**

- **Numbness and shock**
- **Physical reactions**
- **Pining and searching**
- **Poor concentration**
- **Questioning (why? what if?)**
- **Relief**
- **Sorrow and sadness**

Anger

Children often feel and express anger after a death. They are angry at the person who died, angry at the unfairness of what has happened and angry at things changing. Feeling as if things around them are out of control can be scary – and children (and adults) often react to this by getting cross. Strong, angry feelings can be hard to cope with or to put into words and may come out as tantrums or lashing out. They may also feel uncomfortable when other people in the house are distracted or distressed.

Anxiety and fear

It can make a child very anxious and fearful when someone dies, especially if they don't understand what has happened. The world can feel very unsafe if a person can just stop being here. People often say that grief can feel a little like being afraid; a shaky uncertainty because everything has changed. It's very common for children to become clingier and intensely upset at being separated from those around them and for them to need much reassurance – both in words and hugs.

Arguing

It seems as if the death of someone important can lead to a flare up of arguing within the family; it's almost as if a child is arguing with what has happened through arguing with their siblings or parents. This, in turn, can lead a child to feel less safe and secure – and, confusingly, that leads to their being more disruptive: an uncomfortable circle.

Avoidance and denial

Sometimes children can try and push away the idea that someone has died. They may truly not believe it or say they don't believe it. They'll try to avoid any conversations about the person who died and try to stop other people talking too. They are, at a subconscious level, trying to avoid the reality and finality of the death of someone.

Confusion and bewilderment

It is very natural for a child to be confused over what has happened when someone dies. They may struggle with the concept of death, they may be confused by the changes in routine and in those around them, they may be puzzled by their own feelings and responses. Simple, straightforward explanations can begin to reassure.

Disbelief

Even children who understand about death may find it hard to take in that someone has died and will no longer be part of their lives. It is natural for everyone, including adults, to struggle to believe it. This feeling will fade as the reality of their death sinks in but it may take a while before a child stops expecting someone to appear.

Guilt and feeling to blame

Children often wonder if they are to blame for someone dying and assume it must be their fault. They can also feel guilty over remembered times when they said something unkind to the person who died. This can be especially true when a sibling dies, since there will always have been times when the sibling was felt to be annoying. It's important to remind a child that there was nothing they said or did – or didn't say or didn't do – that made this person die.

Hollowed-out

One of the biggest feelings that seems associated with grief is to feel as if you have had a hole punched right through your middle. Adults might find words for this sensation such as 'feeling hollow inside' but children – feeling this for the first time – may not have the words to describe the sinking, breathless, empty feeling. Sometimes they describe it as feeling 'bored' or 'hungry'. It can help to share that you feel something similar and connect it to the grief that comes when someone important has died.

Numbness and shock

Sometimes children say they feel numb after someone has died; the shock seems to have frozen them inside. For some, it can take a while for the pain to break through. It can make it hard to answer well-meaning questions from adults such as 'how are you feeling?', because the honest answer is 'nothing'. Children say it can feel as though they have taken a deep breath in and then can't breathe out and this can make them feel detached from what is going on.

Physical reactions

After someone dies, children sometimes develop physical symptoms which can include tummy aches, sickness, headaches. Occasionally, they may develop symptoms that unconsciously mimic the illness that caused the death (for example, a cough if someone had a lung condition). They may lose their appetite or overeat to try and fill the emptiness inside. They may have trouble getting to or staying asleep – or may be sleepy during the day.

Pining and searching

There is a particular sadness after someone has died that can take the form of a desperate missing or pining for that person. It can be a very physical sensation: wanting to see, touch, hold or smell them and it can feel like a heartbreaking longing for them to return, even for just a moment.

This can also be experienced as wanting to search for the person who died, actually to look for them in places they used to visit in case they will be there. Children and adults also may think they've caught a glimpse of the person or may dream vividly about them.

Poor concentration

Children may lose concentration at school, finding it hard to keep focused when they are feeling really disturbed and upset.

Questioning (why? what if?)

Children are used to asking questions and receiving answers, and may have many questions about what has happened, why it happened and if something could have changed what happened. These can be exhausting but encouraging questions and supplying the best answers you can is so helpful in keeping communication flowing. Their questions reveal what they are thinking or worrying about, and show us that they need a truthful reply.

Relief

It may seem an odd feeling to have here, but sometimes people – including children – can feel relieved when someone dies. This may be because they have been ill for a long time or if everyone has spent a long time worrying that they might die. It's also reasonable (for example, if a sibling has been dying and parents have been preoccupied) to look forwards to regaining attention. Being relieved is a natural response to a long period of tension and stress and does not mean children do not care.

Sorrow and sadness

A feeling of deep sadness is the most frequent response to the death of someone close. Feeling sad can last for years and can sit alongside all other reactions and responses. Sometimes people can be confused if children do not cry after someone has died but some children 'keep their tears on the inside', disliking the feeling of being upset. It may be helpful to share that it can help to cry – to release some of the feelings, at least temporarily. Sometimes children may seem angry or anxious or confused when what they are mainly feeling is deeply sad.

"His dad died when he was almost three; I thought we'd come through but suddenly, when he was about nine, he began to become very upset about him. He was angry that other people in his class had fathers." Lauren

37

PUDDLE JUMPING

It can be helpful to remember that a child's experience of a death in the family and their reactions to it may be different from yours as an adult.

Children often show their feelings through the way they behave – and feelings of grief are no different. This behaviour may also correspond to their age and level of understanding about what has happened.

Younger children may also move quite rapidly from one feeling or one behaviour to the next. A child can seem inconsolable one minute and then be happy and noisy the next. At Winston's Wish, we talk about this as 'puddle jumping' or 'jumping in and out of puddles of grief' to describe the way children grieve.

Adults tend to wade through rivers of grief or can get stuck in vast seas of grief; children hop in and out of puddles. Both adults and children can be surprised by sudden tsunamis of grieving.

"He was like an April day – sunny, then heavy showers of tears, then sunshine again." Rosie

AS TIME PASSES

Not only is grief unique to the individual, it is also experienced differently by each individual as time passes – even within one family. For example, one child may be initially very angry, and later very sad; their sibling might be very fearful and later, very angry. Feelings and thoughts can become more complex and interwoven as time passes.

This can sometimes be shown through behaviours. Children of primary school ages, especially those who are still developing their understanding of the finality of death, may react to someone's disappearance and failure to reappear with either very 'good' or very 'challenging' behaviour (neither labels are fair, of course). This may be a subconscious attempt to get normal life back, to 'reset reality' to a time when everyone was together and happy. ('*Surely if I'm this loud, Mummy will have to come back to tell me to shush?*')

Over time, children may become quieter and refuse to talk about feelings; they may become angrier with shorter fuses, they may become more physical and boisterous. It's really important to keep gently helping them to recognise what is happening, to accept their feelings and to manage the way they express these feelings through their behaviour. One activity that seems to work well for this we call '**Fizzy Feelings**'.

Over time, you have also had the chance to add pieces to complete the picture of what has happened, as children either understand more or have the capacity to hear and learn more. This may lead to deeper discussions about how and why the person died.

As children near the top of primary schools, they will have fully developed their understanding of death and dying; this may bring reawakened grieving for a person who died when they were tiny.

FIZZY FEELINGS

You need two bottles of sparkling water (you could use other fizzy drinks but it gets sticky!) and a place to be, probably outside, that won't get damaged.

Ask your child to start shaking one of the bottles very, very hard. You and other members of the family can take a turn too. While shaking, explain that: '*sometimes feelings get all churned up inside us – fear, worry, anger, confusion (shake, shake, shake). All these feelings are perfectly reasonable to feel when someone has died. But what can happen is that they build up and build up (shake, shake, shake). Then, if you're not careful…*' At this point the person with strongest hands takes the top off quickly – '*they can explode and soak everyone around them.*' Or else, you screw the lid down so hard, you just can't open it up again.

Then take the second bottle and encourage the child to shake this one as hard as possible (shake, shake, shake). While shaking, explain that: '*all those churned up feelings are very natural. It's reasonable to feel angry or anxious. (shake, shake, shake) But we need to find a way to let all those fizzy feelings out without drenching everyone around us…*' At this point, the person with the strongest hands gently and very s - l - o - w - l - y eases the top off the second bottle so no one gets soaked.

Then you can all share your ideas about things that help you express your fizzy feelings without exploding over each other; for example, ideas from your 'Emotional First Aid Kit' (p 60-61).

WHAT CHILDREN MIGHT SAY AND WHAT THEY MIGHT MEAN

While children's behaviour can reveal how they are feeling, children often find this really difficult to put into words. In fact, it can be difficult to extract any information in words (ask most children what happened in school and they'll probably say 'nothing'). Just because your child says 'I'm fine' when you ask how they are feeling, doesn't necessarily mean that they are fine. They might mean: 'I'm OK enough to not want to talk about it right now' or 'I'm really not fine but I don't want to risk expressing it for fear of everything tumbling out.'

Sometimes, adults feel they shouldn't get upset in front of their children and children often tell their parents that they don't want them to express their feelings; for example, they may say 'I don't want you to cry, Mum. I'll leave the room if you cry.'

It's scary and confusing for children to see those closest to them in distress. However, there is a difference between what children want and what they need. They need to see that the grief everyone is feeling is, indeed, immense and is hurting everyone profoundly. And they need to see that while you may howl, you will then be able to make tea, drive to football training, or play a game.

Learning that huge emotions are appropriate and can be safely felt and expressed and then other activities can be resumed is so important. It encourages children to risk opening up to their own feelings about what is happening.

"I thought grief would unite us but it hurt us – and keeps hurting us – in different ways." David

THE 'PROTECTION RACKET'

Parents often want to protect children from how they themselves are feeling and children can often want to avoid adding to their parents' grief by talking about their own. They instinctively want their parents to be happy, so they try to protect them too. A 'protection racket' can develop where everybody is hiding their true feelings – for the kindest of reasons.

Open, honest communication can make everyone feel more secure. It can also make the whole family more relaxed if people aren't constantly trying to behave how they think other people want them to.

"Alice was able to tell me that she didn't want to ask about her mother's death in case it would make me cry and be upset. So I told her that I cry because it is upsetting and I miss her mum. I've told her so often that it's OK for me to cry and that's my way of getting my feelings out. She's only recently realised that it's not her that's making me cry. I'm crying because Erica died. Now Alice brings me tissues..." Luis

"*Losing a (parent) as a child makes you feel disadvantaged emotionally. There isn't that person willing you on, there to help you. No one there to rebel against or draw things from. You become… self-reliant and you grow up quickly in one sense, and never grow up in another.*" James Dyson

THINKING ABOUT YOUR CHILD'S GRIEF

THE UNIQUE FINGERPRINT OF GRIEF – *See page 44*

YOUR CHILD – *See page 45*

WHO DIED? – *See page 49*

HOW DID THEY DIE? – *See page 50*

WHAT ELSE IS HAPPENING? – *See page 52*

THIS FAMILY – *See page 52*

THIS COMMUNITY AND THIS SCHOOL – *See page 53*

THE UNIQUE FINGERPRINT OF GRIEF

The way we experience grief and the way we express our grief is unique to us. Our response is as individual as a fingerprint and this is just as true for children. Even within one family, people will respond in individual ways to a death of someone with whom they had a particular, unique relationship.

There is no right or wrong way to grieve. There is no hierarchy and no competition in grieving. There are no 'oughts' or 'shoulds' when it comes to grief.

When we talk with grieving families at Winston's Wish, we are trying to understand what this particular death means to the individuals in the family; especially to the individual child who has been bereaved. To do this, we look at the impact of the death of this person, in this way, at this time and as part of this family and community on this child. This process may help you to consider the impact on your child.

YOUR CHILD

The most important thing to consider is what makes your child a unique individual, experiencing a unique grief. All the following factors will affect how they grieve:

- **their age**

- **their developmental level of understanding**

- **their special educational and other needs**

- **their gender**

- **their usual level of anxiety**

- **their usual level of resilience.**

"It's like I am carrying a glass of water and I have to hold it very steady and walk very slowly because I daren't spill a drop. Because if I spill even one drop, I'm afraid I'll spill the whole glass. And I can't risk that." Jermaine

AGES AND STAGES

The main emphasis of this book is on supporting grieving children **aged between five and 11** (we have other publications aimed at supporting under-fives and teenagers: see boxes). However, it may be helpful to have some brief ideas about how a child's age may affect their reactions to a death.

Children under five – or with the developmental understanding of a child under five – will:

• experience death as a separation from the person who has died or as having been abandoned by them

• not understand the idea of death and not understand that it is permanent

• keep expecting the return of dead person and keep looking for them

• ask the same questions over and over

• show their feelings in their behaviour and play

• may have more tantrums or meltdowns than usual.

Children from five to eight – or with the developmental understanding of a child under eight – may:

• begin to understand death is forever

• begin to worry about other people dying

• have a growing sense of their own mortality

• be curious about death and dying or see death as 'spooky' or 'scary'

• be confused by what has happened

• think that there is something they can do that might bring back the person who has died (for example, get a ladder to the sky, or wish on a star)

• think they have caused the death by something they did or didn't do

• act in a way that is seen as particularly naughty or particularly good in the hope that the deceased person will come back to tell them off or praise them

• begin to feel different to their friends and peers

• have strong feelings of loss but may lack the words with which to express their feelings.

Our book *Never Too Young To Grieve* is about supporting bereaved children under the age of five.

Children from nine to 11 – or with the developmental understanding of a child under eleven – may:

- understand that being dead lasts for ever and that there is nothing that can bring the person back to life
- begin to understand that everyone will die – including themselves
- be worried about close relatives dying
- be curious about the physical aspects of death and find the subject of death fascinating
- notice how their family differs from those of their peers
- have the words to express how they are feeling but may need encouragement to do so.

Children over 11 – or with the developmental understanding of a child over 11 – will or may:

- have an adult understanding of death
- be more likely to express their grief as adults do but still find themselves becoming overwhelmed
- become aware of the absence of the person who died in the future (for example, that they won't see the child leave school, find a job, have children of their own)
- begin to question the 'meaning of life' and struggle to understand why people have to die ('*What's it all about if we all die anyway?*')
- begin to seek independence but also feel the need for safe dependence
- begin to talk more to their friends than to their family
- feel the pressure to fit in with their peer group so may suppress feelings about or even discussion of the person's death
- sometimes find themselves in the role of 'comforter' or taking on adult responsibilities too young
- explore some risk-taking behaviours (for example, drinking alcohol)
- experience the normal turmoil of adolescence alongside their grief.

Our book *You Just Don't Understand* is about supporting bereaved teenagers.

47

GROWING OLDER

Also, children will understand not only more about death in general but also more about the death of their special person as they grow older. In this way, a child who is bereaved when they are under five will experience their grief in a different way when they are eight and in a different way again when they are 11 and as a teenager.

EDUCATIONAL AND OTHER NEEDS

Children's understanding might be affected by more than their developmental stage; for example, those with autism or other development disorders may show little initial reaction when someone dies. They may surprise by asking very direct questions about the person's body or they may find it challenging to understand other people's expressions of grief. They may become very anxious about changes to previously predictable routines and find the presence of well-meaning visitors overwhelming.

GENDER

You may come across some large generalisations about the ways boys and girls grieve. Society sometimes seems to expect boys not to cry, for example, or girls not to express their anger. Somehow, children can absorb these expectations and express themselves in ways that they feel others expect of them. It's really important to remember that everyone is an individual and there are no 'male' or 'female' ways of grieving – children will appreciate being told this.

ANXIETY AND RESILIENCE

Some children are naturally more anxious than others, worrying over many things at once. Some are more easily able than others to bounce back from setbacks and challenges. Previous experiences may also have contributed to a child's resilience and anxiety, making them more or less able to weather difficulties.

Our book *We All Grieve* is about supporting children with SEND.

"My friends don't really understand about my gran. But she was more like my mum. She was always there for me." Joe

48

WHO DIED?

Who has died and the relationship your child had with this person is also very important in thinking about your particular child's grief. For example:

• if a **father or mother** has died, was the child their 'shadow'/best mate? Did they have a complicated relationship with much arguing? Did the parent live with the family or were they only seen occasionally (or not at all)? Was the person who died a step-parent who was adored or resented?

• if a **grandparent** has died, were they the grandparent who was seen every day after school or the one who lived 400 miles away and rarely visited? Were they the child's critic or the person they confided in?

• if a **sibling** has died, were they the adored big brother or annoying little sister? Was the sibling seen as a rival? Was it the sibling who was always fought with or the one who shared adventures? A resented step- or half-sibling? The sibling who had been ill for so long and taken all parental attention? The sibling who soothed nightmares?

• if a **teacher, sports coach** or **family friend** has died, what role did they play in this child's life? The person who really listened and cared? The one who encouraged a talent? The one who shared the child's interests?

• if a **friend** or **classmate** has died, were they someone who shared snacks and secrets? Someone always up for a game or a giggle?

"It took Jack months to stop looking up at the time his Daddy Paul used to come home. I think the fact he simply went off to work and never came back was so hard to understand." Steve

It is worth noting that, occasionally, the death of **someone well known** can affect children. Examples might be a favourite musician, TV presenter or member of the royal family.

Among the expectations that other people may have is that a child will respond predictably to the death of a particular person; for example, that all children will be affected in the same way by the death of a father. However, relationships are frequently more complicated than a label. It may be that the person's death comes as a kind of relief – and this may be harder to express and harder to experience.

49

HOW DID THEY DIE?

The way in which someone dies can also have an impact on how the child reacts to the death, at least initially.

AN EXPECTED DEATH

If a person has had an illness for a long time and the child has been included in conversations about what is happening, they may feel more prepared when the person dies. And being prepared like this may have provided opportunities to talk with members of the family about death and dying, and about the feelings and thoughts that may come with grief. The child may have had a chance to say goodbye before the person died.

But sometimes children may become used to a person being ill, may not have expected them to actually die, and are very shocked when it happens.

A SUDDEN DEATH

A sudden death (and a death expected by others may still seem unexpected to a child) gives no time to prepare and no time to say goodbye. By its very nature, a sudden death caused by internal damage to part of the body (such as a heart attack or brain haemorrhage) comes with no warning. It may take a child a long time to understand that the person has died and will never again be able to play, laugh, hug. A sudden death brings many 'if only' and 'what if?' thoughts.

Sometimes a death is sudden because of an accident; a natural reaction is to wonder if anyone was at fault. It's a natural reaction to wonder if someone hadn't been driving carefully, if a railing had been regularly checked for safety, if a warning against swimming in a river had been displayed.

A DEATH CAUSED BY A PANDEMIC

When someone dies during a pandemic, all the usual support systems become less available. People may not be able to offer support or hugs in person; the child may not have been able to visit the ill person in hospital nor attend their funeral. It may also feel as if this death is 'one among very many' rather than something unique. Sometimes external circumstances (for example, a perceived delay in response to the crisis or a parent being a key worker) can make a child feel angry or confused.

A DEATH FROM SUBSTANCE USE

When the person who dies has been dependent on drugs or alcohol and this has led to their death, it can be very difficult for a child to understand. The effects of the substances being used may have made living with the person difficult for the child and this may make grieving for them more complicated. A person's death through drugs or drink can be perceived as a choice to allow their health to be damaged, rather than be around for their child who may wonder if they were loved or thought about enough.

> "Sometimes I was a bit jealous of the attention she got when she came into school with no hair after she'd been in hospital. But I never thought there'd be a day when she wouldn't come in again." Ashleigh

A DEATH FROM SUICIDE

When someone close to a child dies by suicide it can complicate how a child will respond to the death. Despite our greater understanding of mental health challenges, it can still be difficult to talk openly about a death by suicide. Families sometimes tell us: *'it would be easier if they'd died of cancer'*. A child whose important person takes their own life can worry if this person had loved them if they could also leave them. They can have endless, unanswerable 'why?' questions. For parents, there can be the anxiety that the child may grow up to think suicide is an option for them too.

A DEATH CAUSED BY SOMEONE ELSE

It can be particularly challenging for a child when someone close to them is killed by someone else; this may be through murder or manslaughter, through an assault or through an act of terrorism. It can make a child feel very vulnerable and also very angry with the person who caused the death. This is complicated if that person has not been identified or charged and very difficult if the person was killed by someone the child knows. If, for example, one parent kills the other and is imprisoned, the child suddenly faces life without both parents.

A DEATH OF A MEMBER OF THE ARMED FORCES OR EMERGENCY SERVICES

When someone dies who is a member of the armed forces or emergency services, there can be a public aspect to the response to their death, especially if the death has been in the line of duty. It can be complicated to feel simultaneously proud of the person but also angry about the situation in which they died.

Equally, the person may be described by other people as a 'hero' or 'heroine', but this is not necessarily how a child has seen this person.

WHEN THE CAUSE OF DEATH IS UNKNOWN

It can be particularly hard, for adults and for children, to accept when (as happens occasionally) the cause of death may never be known. This may happen if a post-mortem cannot establish the cause of death, or if the person's body has not been found. Occasionally, a family may disagree with the cause of death on a death certificate. For children, not having a sense of why and how someone died can make the world seem a less safe place.

"Now we can look at his photo and think about him as a person. He will always be part of our family – regardless of how he died." Clare

WHAT ELSE IS HAPPENING?

In thinking about the impact on a child of the death of a particular person, it is also relevant to consider what else is going on in their life at the same time. For example:

• **are parents separating or divorcing?**

• **is there enough money coming in? Is someone facing the loss of their job?**

• **is someone else ill in the family?**

• **has a pet recently died?**

• **does this child or a sibling have exams?**

• **is this child facing a change of schools? This includes from infant to junior or from junior to secondary – as well as moving to a new school.**

It is also important to recognise that the death of a family member, especially the death of a parent, can bring additional losses for a child. For example:

• **they may need to move house: losing their comforting bedroom, the den in the garden, a kind next door neighbour**

• **they may need to move school: losing their friends, the familiarity of a supportive teacher, a special corner of the playground**

• **they may need to move to a new area: losing their local park, the shopkeeper who always said hello, a club or sports team.**

THIS FAMILY

The way that a family responds to challenges and the way a family communicates will have a large impact on how a child may respond to someone's death. For example:

• **is the family large or now very small?**

• **is there support from friends (especially if the family is small)?**

• **do members of the family find it easy to share their stories and their feelings?**

• **do people choose to spend a lot of time on their own and on mobile devices?**

• **is the family a blended one, with step-siblings and half-siblings finding their ways to live alongside each other?**

• **are the children looked after by a 'kinship carer' – a grandparent, aunt or uncle who are in the role of a parent?**

• **are the children in looked-after care? How long have they been with their foster carer?**

"We moved to be close to my parents. I had to pack up the home we'd made together, the kids had to leave their schools and friends, I had to leave the support network that had grown up around us while she was ill. But I wanted the kids to have more time with me, now more than ever." Leo

THIS COMMUNITY AND THIS SCHOOL

A family's grieving (both as a family unit and as individuals within that family) will also be affected by the way their local communities respond to what has happened. The local community includes neighbours, the family's faith community, a parent's workplace and the child's school. For example:

- do people in the community acknowledge what has happened or try to avoid talking?

- is the family part of a faith community who can support their bereavement? Do people in the community acknowledge the child's grief and the possible questions about belief raised by this death? Do people expect everyone from the same faith to respond in the same ways?

- has this death attracted attention on social media? Has that been helpful or intrusive? Has the child learned details online that the family were hoping to keep quiet?

- has a parent's workplace responded with sensitivity and generosity to a death in the family?

- does the child's school have a bereavement policy in place? Does the school recognise the fundamental role it will play in how a child responds to a death?

YOUR CHILD'S GRIEF

In this section, we have been describing the various factors that may affect the way that an individual child with all their unique responses, feelings and beliefs responds to the death. The meaning that a child can find in what has happened will have an important part to play in how they will live with and through their grief.

To summarise:

What is the meaning...?

- **for this particular child...?**

- **of the death of this particular person...?**

- **through this particular cause of death...?**

- **at this particular time ...?**

- **living as part of this particular family...?**

- **and as part of this particular community...?**

"They reacted so differently to her death but I can see why. They're such different little people." Wes

"*Children need to be given hope for their future so they feel resilient in the present and can take comfort from the past.*" Julie Stokes OBE

WHAT CAN HELP

WHAT HELPS GRIEVING CHILDREN

From thousands of conversations with children and their families, we have learnt what helps children the most after someone dies.

- **Bereavement support:** grieving children need to receive support from family, school and other important people

- **Explanations and information:** about what has happened, is happening and will happen

- **Reassurance:** that they are safe and loved

- **Expressing their feelings and thoughts:** help to find safe ways to share their thoughts and let out some feelings

- **Acknowledgment:** of their loss and the impact on their life

- **Voice in important decisions:** being involved and feeling included

- **Encouragement to remember:** help to remember and know stories about the person who has died

- **Memorials and 'rituals':** to mark certain days

- **Established everyday routines:** alongside a bit of flexibility and chances to have fun

- **Not to blame:** and not responsible for the death

- **Talking and communicating as a family:** sharing and discussing openly

Copies of this Charter can be downloaded from the Winston's Wish website

THE CHARTER FOR BEREAVED CHILDREN

Winston's Wish supports children, young people and their families after the death of a parent or sibling. This charter is based on our conversations with thousands of children and their families, who have told us what gave them hope after bereavement.

B Bereavement support: grieving children need to receive support from family, school and other important people

E Explanations and information: about what has happened, is happening and will happen

R Reassurance: that they are safe and loved

E Expressing their feelings and thoughts: help to find safe ways to share their thoughts and let out some feelings

A Acknowledgment: of their loss and the impact on their life

V Voice in important decisions: being involved and feeling included

E Encouragement to remember: help to remember and know stories about the person who has died

M Memorials and 'rituals': to mark certain days

E Established everyday routines: alongside a bit of flexibility and chances to have fun

N Not to blame: and not responsible for the death

T Talking and communicating as a family: sharing and discussing openly

Helpline: 08088 020 021
winstonswish.org

WINSTON'S WISH
Giving hope to grieving children

Winston's Wish is a Registered Charity (England and Wales) 1061359 (Scotland) SC041140 | 0107-v2.9-20

BEREAVEMENT SUPPORT: grieving children need to receive support from family, school and other important people

This support is best when it recognises them as individuals, with their unique response to what has happened. As outlined on pages 44-53, taking the time to think through what it is like for this individual child to have experienced the death of this person can guide the support that makes the difference. Such support will recognise cultural, faith and other differences. Usually, the best person to know what is most helpful is the child themselves but sometimes they simply won't know and will rely on the adults around them to help. This support can come from a combination of the family and school – with extra support if needed from a child bereavement service.

EXPLANATIONS AND INFORMATION: about what has happened, is happening and will happen

Straightforward (age-appropriate) information about death and dying in general and about this death in particular can help a child begin to understand not only what has happened and why but also what is happening and what will be happening in the future. This, in turn, can help them to make sense of things and feel more secure. If you're not sure then be led by the child; what they're asking and how they're behaving might be clues as to whether or not they are ready to know more.

A grieving child is helped by being gently encouraged to know and to be able to tell the story of what happened. These stories need to be heard by the important people in their lives.

REASSURANCE: that they are safe and loved

At a time of great change, all children need reassurance and a sense of security among what may feel like chaos. For very young children, regular routines (for things like meals and bedtimes) can help as can additional hugs from other caregivers if a parent is distracted by their own grief. School-aged children will also value the reassurance of a normal routine. Maintaining school attendance and other activities they value can help them feel safe. There are some activities that can help a child feel more secure during a time of change and loss.

HOLDING HANDS

One simple way of helping a child feel close to family members who are away, for whatever reason, is to create a sheet of handprints. Family members put one of their hands flat on a piece of paper (it may need to be a sheet of A3) with fingers touching and then draw around the outline of each hand with a different colour pen or crayon for each person. Make a copy for each person who then puts it somewhere safe (for example, folded up in a pocket or school bag). When a child needs to feel close to their family (or indeed, when an adult does…), they take out their copy and place their hand on top of the outline they drew. They can then 'feel' or sense the fingers of the other people touching theirs and reminding them of their continuing closeness.

SPLINKS

A very simple way of helping a child feel close to someone who is apart from them is to sew a secret kiss into the inside of a school jumper, for example. The child can press the kiss – with no one seeing – and feel the connection.

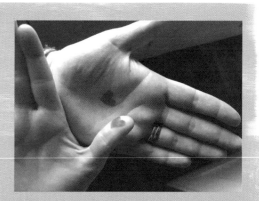

This can be taken further with a 'Splink' – a spot or dot which each person draws on their hand in pen. It may be a tiny dot or a larger heart or a kiss – these two 'Splinks' are pressed together on separation to demonstrate and consolidate the link between the two people and then can be pressed when apart to remember and 'feel' the connection and the continuing love.

"For weeks, I couldn't have a shower or a wee without her sitting outside the door. I understood that she was scared I'd 'disappear' like her dad did but it was so tough. Her gran gave us a ball of wool so she could hold one end and I'd have the other if I went out of sight." Sue

CIRCLES OF SUPPORT

It can also help a child who is feeling insecure after someone has died if they are able to retain a sense of who cares about them and is around to support them.

One way of doing that is to develop a picture of the support that surrounds the child.

We do this sometimes with toys; children can enjoy choosing the right doll or racing car for Grandpa or their best friend's mum. Or you can use a variety of stones or buttons. You can draw the circles on paper, in sand or with ribbons. Afterwards, though, however you have created the picture of the circles of support surrounding the child, it is good to draw it on paper to keep as a reminder.

Start by putting the name of the child (or the toy, pebble, button representing them) in the middle. Draw circles radiating out from them in the centre. Ask them to place on these circles the people they can turn to for support, for care, for attention, for love. In our example, we have included grandparents, the family pet, a best friend and a favourite teacher to give some ideas.

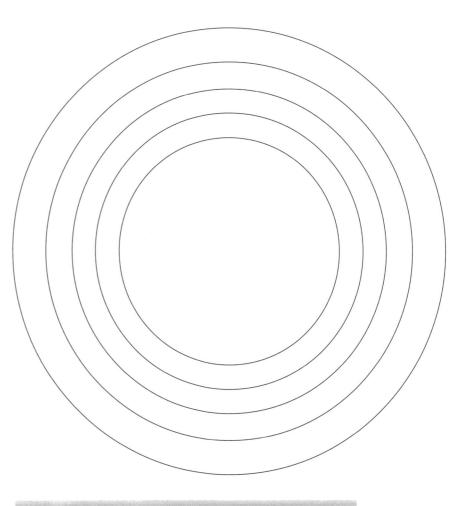

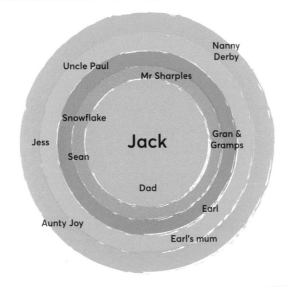

Nanny Derby

Uncle Paul

Mr Sharples

Snowflake

Jess

Jack

Gran & Gramps

Sean

Dad

Aunty Joy

Earl

Earl's mum

"After her other dad died, she needed a lot of reassurance. At bedtime, we'd recite together: 'Daddy loves you; Granny Jo-Jo loves you; Auntie Trish loves you… she was usually asleep before we got to the cat." Dan

EXPRESSING FEELINGS AND THOUGHTS OF GRIEF: help to find safe ways to start their thoughts and let out some feelings

Children may need guidance in how to safely express their feelings, whether this is in words, in actions or through behaviour. Emotions may feel overwhelming and the temptation is to bottle them up – until they either explode or just can't be ignored. There's a helpful activity on page 39 (**Fizzy Feelings**).

They may also need some guidance on what can help when everything feels just a bit too much. Most of us are familiar with First Aid boxes: inside there are boxes and spaces for plasters and creams and bandages – the things that can help soothe the hurts, pains and bumps that can be seen on the **outside**. A **Look after myself First Aid Kit** helps when the hurts, pains and bumps are on the **inside**; a kit that reminds us of what we need when we are feeling overwhelmed, on difficult days or when things build up to bursting point.

This is how we use this idea at Winston's Wish. You can use this template, or draw your own First Aid kit on a piece of paper; it helps to have 8 to 10 boxes of different size and shape. This works best when a child/children complete their own sheets at the same time as their caring adult does.

STEP ONE

Start by sharing a normal First Aid box (if you have one). Talk about the reasons for having a box for the hurts that can be seen. Then explain that people need a similar kit of ideas of things that can help them feel better on difficult days. *'We're each going to have a go at filling a sheet of our own ideas of what can help us feel a little easier and calmer and then we can share them.'*

Each person then draws a picture (and can add words) into each box. It's great to come up with your own ideas but here are some starters:

For children: Hugging a favourite toy; dancing to a favourite upbeat song; eating an apple; speaking to a grandparent; riding a bike; throwing bricks into a box

For young people: Playing a favourite game for half an hour; thumping a cushion; eating pizza; talking to friends on the phone or online; writing down thoughts in a book; listening to music; climbing a tree; eating biscuits

For adults: Bath with bubbles; walk in nature; coffee with friends; favourite bar of chocolate; stroking a cat; playing football

STEP TWO

The next bit is sharing your kits. We suggest leaving one box empty until this stage because the other person usually has a great idea you want to borrow. For example, *'I wish I'd put 'have a hot drink' on mine'*. You are allowed a veto if it's really necessary. For example, the adult could say *'You can't have 'kick the cat' but you could have 'hug the cat and kick a cushion' '*. The child can say in return *'Then you can't have both chocolate AND cake.'*

STEP THREE

Then you find somewhere to put the completed kits so they can be easily accessed. At home, this might be stuck to the fridge with a magnet, or in a drawer.

STEP FOUR

The next stage is using the kits. This may be when someone is feeling very angry or very 'full up'. Getting the First Aid kits and then deciding what idea to use reminds a child or young person that they do have 'strategies' – ways of coping when things threaten to overwhelm them. It could go like this:

'I think we need our First Aid kits… where's mine? Where's yours? Right… well, I can't ring Sally because she'll be at work and I can't have a bath because I'm about to take you to school and I guess red wine is out of the question, so it'll have to be a doughnut! How about you?' 'Can't have pizza for breakfast, guess I can't go on the X-box because it's school time, can't see the cat… I'll kick a football against the wall for five minutes.'

In this way, everyone is gently reminded that they do have their own ways to manage their pressure: the hurts, pains and bumps on the inside.

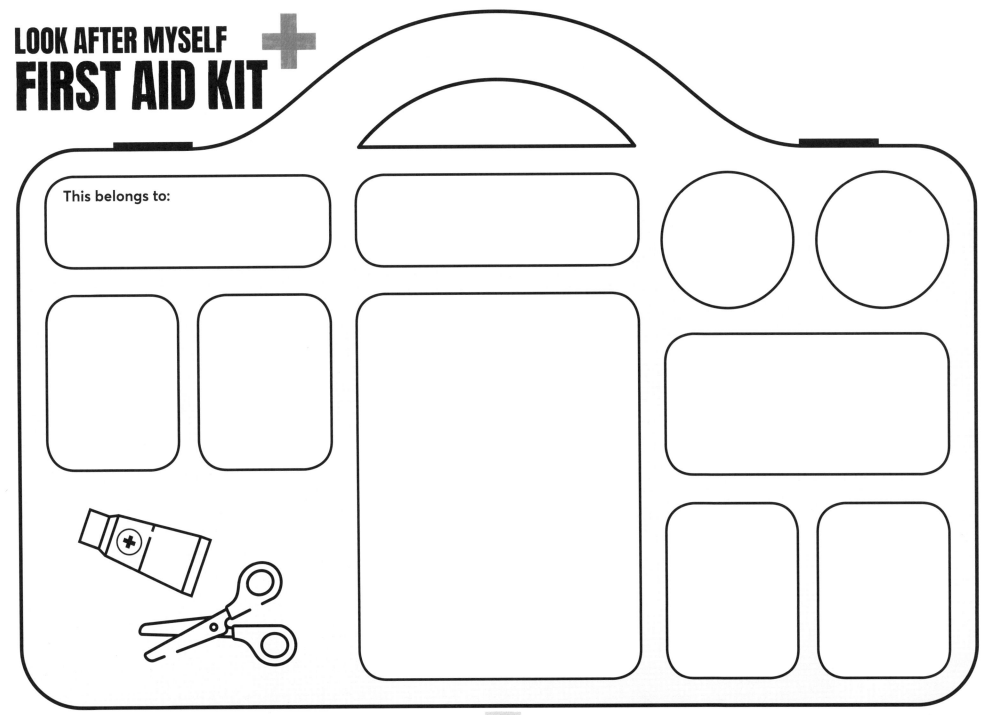

LOOK AFTER MYSELF
FIRST AID KIT

This belongs to:

ACKNOWLEDGMENT: of their loss and the impact on their life

Sometimes people overlook children's grief, maybe from fear of 'making things worse'. Or people don't know what to say – so end up saying nothing. Bereaved children say that one of the most important and helpful things is to acknowledge what has happened. Relatives, friends, teachers can really help by saying something simple such as: *'I'm really sorry to hear that your nan has died'*.

VOICE IN IMPORTANT DECISIONS: being involved and feeling included

Wherever appropriate, children appreciate being involved in what the family is experiencing. For example, it can help children to be included in conversations about the funeral, any memorial service and marking future anniversaries. There's a balance between overloading children with adult concerns and sharing enough that they feel part of things. If you're not sure, then be led by the child; what they're asking and how they're behaving might be clues as to whether or not they are ready to be involved more.

ENCOURAGEMENT TO REMEMBER: help to remember and know stories about the person who has died

Questions about the person and looking at photos and videos are simple ways to encourage children to keep refreshing their memories of the person who died. Younger children may have few memories of the person – or have even been born after the person died – and, for them, stories become a vital part of giving them a vivid sense of the person who lived. In this way, the person's death does not come to define them and children become used to thinking and talking about their life.

Some people gather the memory prompts requested from friends (see page 30) into a jar or box and pull one out occasionally to share. Of course, everyone can write down memories whenever they crop up and contribute them to this memory jar.

Having ways to mark special days and simple, regular reminders of the person who died (for example, lighting a candle once a week) help ease children's worries that they might forget the person who has died. There are some other ideas on how to do this on page 73.

Children will appreciate the chance to assemble a box of memories linked to the person. As time passes, looking over the items in the box helps children reflect on and refresh these memories. For children with few memories, holding, seeing and smelling these items helps them to build a concrete sense of the person who died. Items might include: a piece of jewellery, an item of clothing, a favourite book or CD, shells from a holiday, their aftershave or perfume, tickets from a day out.

"It was helpful for us to find ways to focus on memories of her brother's life rather than keep thinking about his death" Guy

MEMORY BOX

When someone important has died, memories of shared times can be comforting and can help children feel close to the person. One way of doing this is to start building a memory box. Children can be helped and encouraged to add to the memory box themselves.

STEP 1 Fill the memory box with items that are about times spent together or things you have shared. These can include things like a watch, a tie, a scarf, some jewellery. You could include some photographs and cards from birthdays. Some perfume or aftershave? How about a pair of glasses or a favourite CD?

STEP 2 Try and make sure that the things in the box have a story or memory attached

STEP 3 It can really help if the person helping to create the box can write a label for each item to jog memories

STEP 4 Some children like to keep their boxes private, others like to show them to family and friends; it's totally up to you

TOOLKIT

- A box (you could buy one from the Winston's Wish website or you could make your own out of something like a shoebox)

- Some things that trigger memories of times shared, for example: a piece of jewellery, an item of clothing, a favourite book, shells from a holiday, tickets from a day out

- Pens, stickers, glitter etc – if you'd like to personalise your box

"Dad and me once went to watch our team play. The ticket and the programme and a photo of us there all help to remind me of what a great day it was..." Ollie

REMEMBERING GOOD TIMES, ACCEPTING TOUGH TIMES TOO: MEMORY STONES

Of course, it's important to acknowledge that not all memories are easy and comfortable to hold onto. Not all relationships between the person who died and your child will have been harmonious, and it's possible that some memories are complicated and disturbing. At Winston's Wish, we use a simple activity to demonstrate how difficult memories can exist and find their place alongside everyday and special ones.

A simple bag of three stones may be a useful way to have a really meaningful conversation with your children and help them to find a way of coping with all sorts of memories. In every relationship we have, there are ordinary, difficult and special moments. Sometimes it can be hard to find a balance between the difficult memories which are often associated with a death and happier, more positive memories. The three different stones can be used to convey a message in a special and safe way.

The first two stones can usually be found in a garden or park. Gemstones can be found at craft or gift shops. Encourage your children to hold each stone in turn and give examples of memories and events that they would attach to the different stones. You can also share your own.

The **smooth pebble** needs to be ordinary, smooth and round. It feels ordinary and fairly comfortable to hold in your hand. It is there to represent ordinary, everyday memories of the person who died. (*'He had cornflakes for breakfast every single day.' 'She couldn't bear to miss an episode of EastEnders.'*)

The **rough rock** needs to have jagged edges and to feel sharp and painful to hold. It is there to represent the memories of difficult and hard times and also memories of the way that the person died. (*'I remember some of the rows we had; we said some hurtful things to each other.' 'When I close my eyes, I can still see where he died.'*)

The **gemstone** feels precious, rare and polished. It is there to bring back memories of the really special times spent with the person who died. (*'I'll never forget that day on the beach when he built me a boat out of sand. He couldn't stop laughing.' 'One day we dressed up in silly clothes and she let me wear her high heels.'*)

Then explain that the secret is to try to find a way to hold the three stones in your hand at the same time – the rough alongside the precious and the ordinary – and to hold these three types of memories together in a way that they all find their place. What happens is that you have to adjust the stones a bit so that the rough rock is not too obvious or sore; in this way, the rough rock becomes no more important than the other two.

The stones can be stored in a little bag and brought out, for example on a tough day, as a useful way to start a conversation. For example: *'Does the rough rock feel particularly sharp today?'*

MEET OTHERS: not the only one

Some schools have an occasional lunchtime group for children who have been bereaved or who are going through big changes (such as family breakdown or serious illness). Children may feel that they are the only people who have had someone important die and it reduces a sense of isolation to meet others in the same situation.

MEMORIALS AND RITUALS: to mark certain days

Sometimes children can worry that they (or others) will forget the person who has died. They are reassured by the regular marking of special days, such as the person's birthday or the anniversary of the day they died. Some ideas for marking such days can be found on pages 72-73. Having the choice to participate in other events that mark the person's life or death (such as occasionally visiting the grave or somewhere that reminds the child of the person who died) can be helpful for some children (and can become burdensome for others).

Sometimes, a regular 'ritual', such as lighting a candle by the person's photograph at a fixed time each week (for example, 6pm on a Monday) can be both reassuring and a helpful focus for expressing any worries or difficult emotions. This provides a chance for the family to stop briefly to remember and share any thoughts.

ESTABLISHED EVERYDAY ROUTINES: alongside a bit of flexibility and chances to have fun

When someone dies, it's really tough to keep things on track. Sometimes, regular routines go out of the window and, sometimes, to keep things exactly the same as before seems the best way of getting through. Children who are grieving feel comforted when routines are recognisably the same – but it's also important to feel that things can be flexible if needed. For example, this might mean staying up a bit longer to talk through some worries, delaying tea to finish watching Mum's favourite film. It's a blend of regularity and flexibility that's **'just right'**.

It may seem a surprising thing to include in a list of helpful things for grieving children but it is really important that children are allowed and even encouraged to continue to enjoy their childhood. There can be plenty of time for sorrow, remembering, hurting – but it's important to balance this with time for fun, too. Children need some 'down time' when all that is required is to kick a ball, splash water about or laugh very loudly.

NOT TO BLAME: and not responsible for the death

Children often wonder if they are to blame for someone dying and assume it must be their fault. It is hugely important to ensure that children are told that they are not responsible for the death – it is not their fault. Nothing they said or did – or didn't say or didn't do – caused this person to die.

TALKING AND COMMUNICATING AS A FAMILY: sharing and discussing openly

Open communication within the family helps children understand what has happened and helps them feel comfortable sharing how they are feeling. This includes seeing adults around them express their own emotions and for those adults to encourage talk about the person who has died.

Family members might take it in turns to ask each other questions. For example: *'What was Del's favourite colour?' 'What was the funniest thing Del ever did?' 'What's the first thing you think of when I say Del's name?' 'What were Del's favourite sort of crisps?'*

"I tried not to cry in front of her and then I wondered why she didn't seem upset that her nan had died. Things were easier when we told each other we were crying in private. Now we share our grief." Jude

SOME THINGS TO TRY TO AVOID

Children tell us that these are some of the least helpful responses from people after someone has died:

- silence / lack of acknowledgment of what has happened

- someone changing the subject when the death is mentioned

- being told how they are feeling (*'You must be feeling so…'*)

- having their grief compared to someone else's (*'I know how you feel, my cat died'*)

- false reassurance (*'time heals'*)

- being told to *'cheer up'*

- being told that you should feel better 'by now' just because the death was several months or years ago?

- being told they are *'the man of the house now'* or *'such a help to your mother as the eldest'*

- having their names left off condolence cards and letters

- feeling that everyone else has forgotten the person who died

HOW SCHOOLS CAN SUPPORT GRIEVING CHILDREN

Schools and their staff have such an important role to play in supporting children's grief; this is particularly true at the primary school level where familiar class teachers and well-known teaching assistants are a crucial part of a child's support system and their daily world.

RETURNING TO SCHOOL AFTER A BEREAVEMENT

When a school learns about a death, it may be only hours after the child knows. It is really helpful for someone in leadership and/or the child's class teacher to contact the family. This could be by phone or in person and can be followed up with a card for the child. This is:

- **partly to express the school's shock and sadness at what has happened**

- **partly to communicate that the school will do all they can to support the child who has been bereaved**

- **partly to plan how (and when) that child will return to school.**

School provides a familiar, routine part of children's lives. Many children who have been bereaved find returning to school comforting, even quite soon after someone has died, because it shows that some things are reliable and stay the same – even if so much else is changing. If the child stays away from school for a long time, it can be harder for them to return and it may be harder for them to pick up their friendships. This in turn may make a child feel more isolated and alone.

It can really help a child return to school if their class teacher and maybe a friend meet them outside. It is also helpful if the child can be present when the class teacher simply reminds the class what has been happening and gives them a few prompts for action. For example: *'We have Alfie back with us today. As you know, Alfie's mum died last week. She'd been ill for a long time but it's still a huge shock for Alfie and his dad. Alfie has asked me to say that he's really grateful for all the kind messages people have been sending but it's still a bit hard for him to talk about it. So, do include him in your games but also give him a bit of space to find his feet, OK?'*

It is normal for bereaved children to find it hard to concentrate after someone has died. They may also become overwhelmed – and then '**puddle jump**' back to laughing with a friend. They may want everything to be as normal as possible or they may need people to acknowledge regularly that things have changed forever.

"When they heard what had happened, all the children in the class asked to send notes home to Michael. Some even shared their own experience of loss; they said they missed Michael and wanted him back in goal! He read the notes and decided to come back to school the next day. I guess he knew they cared about his dad's death but importantly he also knew he would be treated as normal." Tim, Year 4 teacher

WHAT HELPS A GRIEVING CHILD IN SCHOOL?

Some simple things can have a significant effect on how grieving children feel supported at school. These are some of the things they say are helpful:

• **acknowledging what has happened** (*'I am so sorry to hear that your mum has died.'*)

• **nominating a particular person to be their lead supporter (this may be the class teacher or another person with a welfare role)**

• **having a plan for when things may become overwhelming**

• **having some ideas on how to support the child to separate from their parent or carer at the start of the day (for example, a 'Splink' or handprint see page 58)**

• **being alert for any assumptions that the chid 'is doing fine' or 'understands what has happened' – it's always worth checking**

• **keeping alert for subjects in the curriculum that may need some sensitive handling, for example:**

   - **finding ways to include the child comfortably in any Mother's or Father's Day activities or**

   - **thinking about how Egyptian 'mummies' are discussed**

• **keeping a calendar of important dates for this child (for example, the birthday or date of death of the person who died).**

When a child is bereaved and the school community becomes aware, it can be challenging for other children who have previously been bereaved. It may reawaken their own grieving or prompt new questions. It is helpful if staff can be alert to all those who have been bereaved.

Teachers at the top of primary schools can make the transition to secondary school so much easier for children if they ensure that the new school is aware of any bereavements, along with any important dates for the children in question. They may also be able to play a role in any difficulties around allocations to secondary schools that may affect bereaved children.

Schools who support grieving children find that the skills that staff and students develop transfer to other areas of life and lead to a community better able to cope with all kinds of adversities.

"I still remember the chemistry teacher coming up to me in the corridor and just saying 'Lisa, I'm so sorry about your mum. You know where to find me if it's a rough day'. I didn't even take chemistry. I'll never forget him doing that." Lisa

CONTINUING SUPPORT FROM SCHOOLS

Schools form a very important part of the partnership of support for a child who is grieving. The routine and everyday familiarity of being at school can be comforting among much change at home. However, there will also be times when a child just can't concentrate, or feelings become just too big and loud.

For such times, it can also be helpful for the child to have a separate 'Look after myself First Aid Kit' specially for use in school (see pages 60-61). This can be created with a class teacher and have some agreed strategies on it to help them on days when things feel too much. This can be kept in a book tray or school bag.

Schools want to do the best for their pupils and support from the whole community is so important to grieving children.

- **many schools have a bereavement policy, but if your school does not have one, you can download a template for a bereavement policy from the Winston's Wish website**

- **we also have a pack for schools that includes sample lesson plans, booklists and other helpful cues**

- **we have free online training for teachers**

- **we hold regular study days for a more detailed look at how to support grieving children**

- **we have PSHE lesson plans and resources for teachers available on the Winston's Wish website**

- **Our Freephone Helpline (08088 020 021) can be contacted for any and all enquiries on how best to support an individual child or children.**

LOOK AFTER MYSELF FIRST AID KIT FOR SCHOOL

Ideas could include:

- **running around the playground three times**

- **five minutes hugging the class mascot**

- **a drink of water**

- **five minutes in the book corner**

- **tearing a scrap piece of paper into shreds (over a bin!)**

- **touching a piece of the natural world (leaf, flower, rabbit, grass)**

- **using all five senses: see something, smell something, hear something, taste something, touch something**

"I wanted to support him in any way I could but wasn't sure how to do this. The training helped me understand where to start" Helen, Year 6 teacher

"*There is a continuing bond and an ongoing relationship between the bereaved and the person who has died, a bond that is not broken by the fact of death.*" Dennis Klass

LOOKING AHEAD

LOOKING AHEAD

The reality that someone important has died will always be part of your child's life; as we said earlier, it's 'Bear Hunt' territory (**'Can't get over it, can't get under it, can't get round it, got to go through it…'**). However, we know that – with the right help and support, at the right time – bereaved children will go on to live lives full of richness and hope.

As your child grows and develops a deeper understanding of living and dying and of their own place in the world in relation to others, they will revisit their grief in different ways and at different times.

REMEMBERING ON SPECIAL DAYS

It may come naturally to have some regular way of remembering the person for as long as you wish. Some families light a candle every Sunday evening and spend a few minutes just thinking about the person who died.

For all grieving children, certain days can be especially challenging. Marking Mother's Day or Father's Day, for example, can feel really difficult when a parent has died; shops are full of reminders and friends are making cards for their mum or dad. The birthday of the person who died or the anniversary of the death can be very moving.

Christmas and other religious festivals may have been a time where families came together and built special traditions. There may be some traditions that you decide as a family that you want to uphold and others you may wish to change slightly.

On days like these, it is important to look after yourself. Give yourself permission to not be OK and, equally, to smile.

Of course, each anniversary doesn't have to contain a grand gesture; in fact, some families decide to 'write off' some days if they feel there is already enough space given to remembering.

There may be future life events when the person who has died is very much missed. There are ways to invoke their memory; for example, by having photographs of the person who died in a special place on a wedding day.

Some of the following ideas can be used on Mother's Day or Father's Day, on the anniversary of the death or the person's birthday, or, indeed, on any day.

You could mark special days by:

- taking a card, drawing or a special message to their grave, or to where their ashes were buried or scattered

- visiting a place with special memories (for example, the place where you had your best holiday ever) or…

- … visiting a place that you went to regularly (for example, the park or the swimming pool) or…

- … creating a new special place (for example, in the garden of a new house)

- holding a small ceremony with specially chosen music, poems and tributes

- planting some bulbs or a shrub in a place that holds special memories

- bringing a picnic to share that includes some of the favourite food of the person who died (Marmite sandwiches? Chocolate cake? Samosas?)

- bringing something to leave in this 'special place' – maybe some flowers or a poem (laminated if possible)

- writing a letter or a poem: it could start with something like *'I have something I'd like to tell you…'*

- lighting a candle at home by a photograph of the person who died and sharing special memories with each other, while eating the person's favourite takeaway

- listening to their favourite music or watching their favourite film

- trying one of the things the person enjoyed doing: bike riding, gardening, cooking

- looking through a memory box or a memory jar to remember some stories – or starting a collection by asking other people for their memories of the person who died (for example: *'What was the funniest thing they did?' 'I remember the day Jim got stuck on the school roof after climbing up to get his ball.'*)

"They can surprise me by suddenly remembering something I think they've forgotten. Kieran remembered a walk to collect conkers when their dad came too." Lena

Some past theories of how people grieve describe different 'stages of grief' – as if everyone's grief follows the same path and that there is a 'right' way to grieve. We prefer to look at it another way: after talking to many thousands of bereaved families, the way of looking at grief that makes the most sense to us is the idea of **'growing around grief'**. Older theories seemed to suggest that there is a time limit or natural progression to grieving: you'll have heard people say something like 'time heals', suggesting that grief gets smaller.

However, bereaved people's experiences suggest that, actually, grief doesn't go away, it doesn't even grow smaller – we grow larger around it.

And this isn't straightforward either, some days there's space for new experiences and optimistic feelings; some days, it is all grief. However, in time, there seems to be more hope.

Tonkin, L. Growing around grief - another way of looking at grief and recovery. Bereavement Care Volume 5, 1996, Issue 1

WHEN MORE SUPPORT MAY BE NEEDED

To grieve when someone important has died is the most natural thing to do. Most families can cope with a death and, if they can talk about what is happening and how they feel about it, often surprise themselves by how well they cope.

Parents sometimes think that their children need professional help as soon as someone dies. This may be because they feel helpless faced with children's reactions to the news. However, it is not always helpful to pass on the message that outside help from 'professionals' is necessary when a crisis happens. Many families somehow find the resources to support each other, even through the most difficult of times.

However, some difficulties may persist or begin to seriously affect a child's ability to withstand what is happening. They may have daily difficulties in managing their emotions, particularly their anger. They may revert to some things from earlier years such as bedwetting or soiling, nightmares, needing comfort blankets. They may withdraw from activities they previously enjoyed and find it hard to be at school or to concentrate when they are there. Most of these are common and natural. However, if concerns continue over a prolonged period, more help may be needed.

Our Freephone Helpline (08088 020 021) can offer guidance and can help you decide if it is time to seek some additional support and where this might be most appropriately found.

"I always thought of us as four sides of a square. When he died, it felt as if there was a huge gap where his side had been. Gradually, we became a triangle. But the children helped me to see that we were actually a pyramid, made of three strong sides with him as a focal point above, still holding us all together." Faye

AN ALTERED FUTURE

LOOKING AFTER YOURSELF

On aeroplanes, the safety demonstration reminds us to: *'Put your own oxygen mask on before helping others'*. This is because you can't support others if you are overwhelmed yourself. This is also true of supporting bereaved members of your family – you need to look after yourself or you're going to be less able to look after them. We appreciate that this is easier said than done when everything is up in the air after someone has died and you are experiencing your own grief.

Supporting grieving children – even if you have not been bereaved yourself – can be physically draining and emotionally demanding, bringing up memories and pains from previous losses. Your child does not need you to be a 'super parent' but does need you to be able to take care of them and to have some space to listen and some time to play.

It can help to remember the things in your own Look after myself First Aid Kit (see page 61) that give you that important chance to draw breath, feel grounded and listen to your own feelings and your own grief. Try to remember that you are doing the very best you can in exceptionally challenging circumstances.

LOOKING FORWARD WITH HOPE

We started by saying that everyone grieves differently, including children. If anyone tells you that you or your child 'should' be doing this or feeling that, remind them of the uniqueness of your grief. (You could lend them this book.) Grieving for someone important has a definite start point but no definite end point. The truth is that you and your child will always carry what has happened inside you.

There will be days when, on waking up, your child – and you – will forget what has happened for a few seconds, and feel guilty for having done so. Then there will be days when, for a while, they can laugh with a friend, enjoy a programme on TV or kick a ball about.

One day you will find that your child – and you – remember and think more about the life of the person who died than about the fact that they died. Neither of you will forget that, but it will seem less vivid than who they were and what you shared with them while they were alive.

Above all, we hope that the ideas and suggestions in this book will help to make it possible for your family to live through and beyond what is happening.

With the right help and support, your child will find their way to an altered future; one which is resilient and fulfilling and enriched by having shared this profound experience with those close to them.

Image has been reproduced with kind permission from Gary Andrews @garyscribbler

BOOKS AND RESOURCES

I MISS YOU: A FIRST LOOK AT DEATH

By Pat Thomas. Illustrated by Lesley Harker

A very simple and straightforward book about death and dying aimed at pre-school children. (Ages 2 to 5)

MISSING MUMMY

By Rebecca Cobb

This lovely book looks at the loss of a parent from a child's perspective, exploring the many emotions a young child may experience. (Ages 3 to 7)

IS DADDY COMING BACK IN A MINUTE?

By Elke Barber and Alex Barber

This book provides reassurance and understanding through clear and honest answers to the questions a boy raises after his father's sudden death. (Ages 3 to 7)

ALWAYS AND FOREVER

By Alan Durant. Illustrated by Debi Gliori

A gentle story about the differing ways Fox's friends react to his death and what helps them remember him. (Ages 4 to 9)

BENNY'S HAT

By Juliet Claire Bell. Illustrated by Dave Gray

A beautiful, honest and gentle book about the death of an older sibling. (Ages 4 to 10)

STEWART'S TREE

By Cathy Campbell

A gentle story for children when a sibling dies shortly after birth.

WHY DO THINGS DIE?

By Katie Daynes. Illustrated by Christine Pym

This engaging lift-the-flap book offers simple answers to the sort of questions all children ask about death, dying, grief, and feelings. (Ages 3 to 8)

WHEN DINOSAURS DIE: A GUIDE TO UNDERSTANDING DEATH

By Laurie Krasny Brown and Marc Brown

This factual book uses cartoon dinosaurs to explain death in a simple and non-threatening way. (Ages 4 to 9)

LIFETIMES: A BEAUTIFUL WAY TO EXPLAIN DEATH TO CHILDREN

By Bryan Mellonie. Illustrated by Robert Ingpen

A simple, gentle explanation of death that talks about beginnings of life, the endings of life and the living in-between. (Ages 4 to 9)

WHERE IS UNCLE AL?

By Eva Hibbs. Illustrated by Sarah Harrison

Featuring a child whose uncle died before she was born, this book could help with conversations about death and beliefs about life. (Ages 5 to 9)

A SHELTER FOR SADNESS

By Anne Booth and David Litchfield

A beautiful, poignant and heart-warming book about creating a shelter for sadness and allowing it space to simply be. (Ages 5 to 99)

SAD BOOK

By Michael Rosen. Illustrated by Quentin Blake

This book is wonderfully honest and will appeal to adults and children of all ages; it explores what 'sad' means, how it affects us and how to cope with it. (Ages 5 to 99)

THE COPPER TREE

By Hilary Robinson. Illustrated by Mandy Stanley

An engaging story about a primary class whose teacher becomes ill and dies. (Ages 5 to 9)

THE INVISIBLE STRING

By Patrice Karst. Illustrated by Joanne Lew-Vriethoff

A beautiful way of reassuring children about the enduring connections between people who love and care about each other, even when apart. (Ages 5 to 11)

HUGE BAG OF WORRIES

By Virginia Ironside. Illustrated by Frank Rodgers

This book explores how a child's worries can build up – and how they can be relieved. (Ages 5 to 10)

SUPPORT FOR PARENTS AND CARERS

In addition to the support Winston's Wish can offer your family, you may appreciate some support for your own grief.

Cruse is the leading bereavement organisation for adults: **www.cruse.org.uk** or **www.crusescotland.org.uk**. They have a network of local branches where trained volunteers offer grief support. A few branches have volunteers trained to work with children and young people. Their Helpline is: **0808 808 1677**

WAY is a support organisation for those who have been widowed while aged under 50: **www.widowedandyoung.org.uk**

Child Death Helpline is for anyone grieving the death of a child of any age: **www.childdeathhelpline.org.uk**. Their helpline is: **0800 282 986**

The Compassionate Friends has a network of local groups for parents grieving the death of a child of any age: **www.tcf.org.uk**

Support After Suicide has information and links to local support (for example, branches of SOBS (Survivors of Bereavement by Suicide)). The website also has a very useful and supportive booklet for anyone affected by suicide: **www.supportaftersuicide.org.uk/help-is-at-hand/**

WINSTON'S WISH RESOURCES

All of these can be purchased from **www.winstonswish.org/shop**

MUDDLES, PUDDLES AND SUNSHINE
A colourful and engaging activity book for children (age five to 10) to complete with support from an adult.

NEVER TOO YOUNG TO GRIEVE
Our book about supporting children under five.

YOU JUST DON'T UNDERSTAND
Our book about supporting teenagers.

WE ALL GRIEVE
Our book about supporting children with special educational needs.

BEYOND THE ROUGH ROCK
Our book about supporting children bereaved by suicide.

HOPE BEYOND THE HEADLINES
Our book about supporting children bereaved through murder or manslaughter.

AS BIG AS IT GETS
Our book about supporting children when someone is seriously ill.

MEMORY BOXES
Beautiful boxes where a child can keep items that spark memories of the person who died.

A POCKET FULL OF PLASTERS
A credit card sized unfolding set of reminders for children of what can help on difficult days.

MILLY'S BUG NUT
By Jilly Janney
Simple story of a family finding their way through bereavement.